HUMOROUS STORIES ABOUT THE HUMAN CONDITION

AN INDEXED COLLECTION OF ANECDOTES

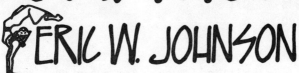ERIC W. JOHNSON

PROMETHEUS BOOKS
BUFFALO, NEW YORK

HUMOROUS STORIES ABOUT THE HUMAN CONDITION: AN INDEXED COLLECTION OF ANECDOTES. Copyright © 1991 by Eric W. Johnson. All rights reserved. No part of this book may be reproduced in any manner whatsoever without written permission, except in the case of brief quotations embodied in critical articles and reviews. Inquiries should be addressed to Prometheus Books, 700 E. Amherst Street, Buffalo, New York 14215, 716-837-2475.

95 94 93 92 91   5 4 3 2 1

Library of Congress Cataloging-in-Publication Data

Humorous stories about the human condition : an indexed collection of anecdotes / [compiled by] Eric W. Johnson.
    p.   cm.
  ISBN 0-87975-651-9
  1. Anecdotes. 2. Wit and humor. I. Johnson, Eric W.
PN6261.H844   1991
818'.02—dc20   90-26321
                                                                                CIP

Printed in the United States of America on acid-free paper.

With gratitude for the joy and humor they have brought into my life, and the lives of thousands of others, I dedicate this book to Joel Goodman, Ph.D., Director of the Humor Project and editor of *Laughing Matters*, and to Bernie Siegel, author of *Love, Medicine and Miracles*.

Some Other Books by Eric Johnson

Textbooks

Improve Your Own Spelling
Language for Daily Use (with Mildred A. Dawson)
How to Achieve Competence in English
Learning to Achieve: the Basic Basic (with Prof. David C. McClelland)
You Are the Editor
English Handbook: How to Read, Speak, and Write Well

Trade Books

How to Live through Junior High School
How to Live with Parents and Teachers
Teaching School: Points Picked Up
Raising Children to Achieve: a Guide for Motivating Success in School and Life
Love and Sex in Plain Language
Love and Sex and Growing Up
Sex: Telling It Straight
People, Love, Sex, and Families
The Family Book about Sexuality (with Dr. Mary Calderone)
An Introduction to Jesus of Nazareth: a Book of Information and a Harmony of the Gospels
Older and Wiser: Wit, Wisdom, and Spirited Advice from the Older Generation
A Treasury of Humor: an Indexed Collection of Anecdotes
The Stolen Ruler
Escape into the Zoo

Contents

Introduction
    (Stories 1-2) 9

1. Human Behavior and Personal Relations
    (Stories 3-48) 13

2. Education, Teachers, and Teaching
    (Stories 49-79) 28

3. Signs of Life—I
    (Stories 80-81) 40

4. Language: What Words Can Do For and To Us
    (Stories 82-143) 42

5. Family Relations
    (Stories 144-170) 65

6. Married Life and Children
    (Stories 171-197) 72

7. Smart Kid Answers—I
    (Stories 198-207) 80

8. Sex
    (Stories 208-233) 83

9. Problems of Life
    (Stories 234-267) 92

10. Signs of Life—II
    (Stories 268-271) 104

CONTENTS

11. Politics, Government, Bureaucracy, and Law
    (Stories 272-301) 107

12. Speakers and Their Speaking
    (Stories 302-315) 122

13. Smart Kid Answers—II
    (Stories 316-324) 127

14. Religion, In and Out of Church
    (Stories 325-376) 130

15. Money and Fund-Raising
    (Stories 377-386) 149

16. Signs of Life—III
    (Stories 387-388) 153

17. Business
    (Stories 389-418) 155

18. The Military
    (Stories 419-428) 166

19. Smart Kid Answers—III
    (Stories 429-437) 170

20. History and Perspective
    (Stories 438-460) 173

21. Old Age
    (Stories 461-475) 180

22. Manners, Good and Bad
    (Stories 476-490) 187

23. Signs of Life—IV
    (Stories 491-493) 193

24. Art and Artists
    (Stories 494-504) 196

25. Writing and Writers: Good and Bad, All Generations
    (Stories 505-521) 201

Index 1. Subjects 211

Index 2. Famous People and Celebrities 227

Introduction

Humor is a distinctly human characteristic. Of all the creatures in the animal kingdom, human beings are the only ones that can laugh. Dogs can act friendly by wagging their tails and nuzzling with their snouts, but such behavior would never be described as a form of humor. Likewise, a cat's meow or purr might be termed cozy, or even amusing, but not truly humorous. Humor requires intellect and a sense of perspective. It's the flip side of tragedy; it makes life bearable and much of it joyous. As George Burns once said in the middle of a story, "Stop laughing and listen." That's the first requirement of this book—read and listen, and go ahead and laugh, too. (But it's not required.)

As I said in my first book on humor, *A Treasury of Humor* (Prometheus Books, 1989), the problem with publishing humorous stories is that nobody really knows where each story comes from, except those based on personal experience. Humorous stories are told and retold, orally or in writing, and the source is soon lost. They fly off and hover around like seagulls looking for their next perch—which reminds me of a pertinent story:

1. Two elderly men, supposedly senile, were committed to an institutional home, located near the sea. One morning they were taken out for a walk by an attendant named Albert. As they strolled along the shore, a seagull flew low and deposited its droppings right on the top of the bald head of one of the elders. Startled by what had just happened, Albert shouted with great concern, "Wait right here. I'll get some toilet paper!" And he ran toward the building.

The one old man then turned to the other, pointing to Albert, and said, "He's a darned fool. That seagull will be a mile away by the time Albert gets back with the toilet paper."

Stories are passed on from person to person until they are just voices from a distant, unreachable source—like the voice of Herbert in the next story:

2. Ernest and Herbert were old men who had been lifelong friends. Though skeptics by nature they still had a little bit of religious faith. They made an agreement that whoever died first would exert every effort to communicate with the other. Herbert was the first to "depart." For many months, Ernest kept alert, hoping to hear from him. Finally, one night he was awakened from a deep sleep by a familiar voice calling, "Ernest! Ernest!"

"Herbert!" cried Ernest. "You've done it! I heard you! Tell me—what's it like?"

"Well, it's not bad," said Herbert. "I'm in a very comfortable, calm, dark place. After a good sleep, I come out everyday and eat in beautiful green meadows. Then I have wonderful sex and go back into my dark comfort. After a short nap, I again feel hungry; so I have some more lovely green food to eat, and more delightful sex, and then it's back again to sleep."

"Golly," said Ernest, "so that's what Heaven is like!"

"Heaven?" said Herbert. "Who said I was in Heaven? I'm a rabbit in Altoona, Pa."

What sorts of people will enjoy this book and find it useful and joy-giving? Anyone who wants to be entertaining, to be entertained, to make a point memorably, to spice up a conversation, and even to enjoy marriage more. This includes conference speakers, teachers, preachers, lawyers, lecturers, doctors, partygoers, before/during/after-dinner speakers, and anyone who enjoys the orgasmic pleasure of leading up to a laugh and then hearing it burst forth.

A Note on Format

This book is organized by chapters, each with a title. However—and it's a *big* however—there is a great deal of overlapping of subject matter. For example, chapter 1 is titled *Human Behavior and Personal Relations,* but *all* of the chapters, in a way, fall into this broad category. Glance down the list of titles. Business, sex, education, manners, old age, smart kids, politics, the military, etc., are all a part of how we human beings behave. So be sure to use the subject index to give you more detailed information about where to find the stories you need.

A Note on the Indexes

This book has two indexes:

Index 1: Subjects
Most of the stories have several subjects, not just one. So if you want a story on religion, sex, used cars, angels, sheep, goldfish, acronyms, or liars, etc., look in the Subject Index.

Index 2: Famous People and Celebrities
Some stories refer to or quote from famous, moderately famous, or a few infamous people. You may want to look up people you are interested in and see what humorous things they have said or written about the human condition.

1

Human Behavior and Personal Relations

Viewpoints: Flies, Philosophers, and Texans

Perhaps the best way to understand our own species is to look at ourselves from the perspective of another species.

> **3.** Two flies were strolling across the ceiling of a rich man's house, discussing what strange creatures human beings are.
>
> The first fly asked, "Have you ever noticed the ceilings of people's houses?" The second fly shrugged, "Yeah, so what?"
>
> "Well, they spend so much money to make their ceilings beautiful, and then they walk on the floor!"

So say the flies. Now let's move to a more sophisticated viewpoint.

> **4.** Socrates (469–399 B.C.), the great Greek philosopher of Athens, is generally regarded as one of the wisest men of all time. He left no writings, but many others wrote down what he said.
>
> Today, we tend to think that the world is going to the dogs, especially the children. Sentiments weren't much different 2400 years ago. Socrates complained:
>
> The children now love luxury; they have bad manners, contempt for authority; they show disrespect for their elders and prefer chatter to exercise. They contradict their parents,

prattle before company, gobble up dainties at the table, cross their legs, and tyrannize over their teachers.

It seems that the world's problems are eternal. But let's keep trying!

Yet another way to get perspective on ourselves is to see how one group of us interacts with another.

5. Texans are frequently teased for their boastfulness about their state. I'm very fond of Texans, but I can't resist telling a story that pokes fun at them. A Texas farmer, named Luke, was visiting a farm in Australia. His host, Malcolm, was showing him around when Luke asked, "Mal, what's growing in that field?"

"Watermelons," replied Malcolm.

"Really?" said Luke. "Why in Texas we grow potatoes bigger than that. Oh, and what's on those trees?"

"Apples, of course," replied host Malcolm.

"Apples?" snorted Luke. "Why Texan *grapes* are bigger than that."

Just then, three kangeroos happened by very fast, and the Texan was startled. "What in God's name were those?"

To which Malcolm calmly responded, "Oh don't you have grasshoppers in Texas?"

National Perspectives

6. One must be careful not to make generalizations about nationalities, but some of them are humorous. For instance, when you ask what category of people are most likely to go to heaven, the French say lovers; the Germans say engineers; and the British say humorists. And who is most likely to go to hell? The French say engineers; the Germans say humorists; and the British say lovers.

So draw your own conclusions about heaven, hell, and the three nationalities—and then try the question on others. If you tabulate enough answers, perhaps you'll be able to say those bleak, awful, self-justifying words: "Studies show that . . . ."

7. Mt. Vesuvius, seven miles from Naples, Italy, is probably the world's most famous volcano. It has erupted many times, and once, in 1631, over 18,000 people were killed. Two American tourists were recently with a group looking over the rim of Vesuvius. One said to the other, "My God! It sure is deep and hot! Reminds you of hell, doesn't it?"

A local guide, hearing the remark, whispered to another European next to him, "These Americans! They've been everywhere."

Threats: Veiled, Unveiled, and Imagined

So much for Homo sapiens—wise mankind—as observed from various distances. Now what about the way we threaten each other, directly or indirectly?

8. Newspaper editors have a challenging but tough life. Often they receive abusive letters or outright threats after taking a position on controversial issues. One editor grew weary of all this, so he ran the Ten Commandments as an editorial. It wasn't long before he received the following terse letter:

Editor:
Cancel my subscription. You're getting too personal.

9. I suppose the most refined and civilized form of threatening behavior is the thrust and parry of vigorous, well-argued debate, especially on important subjects. But even intellectual debate can sometimes degenerate into "rhetorical hooliganism." This term was coined by Bill Muehl, a lawyer who became a clergyman and then a teacher at Yale. He was known for his debating skill. When he was at the University of Michigan, he and his debating partner, a man named Huston, were described as:

... the perfectly balanced team. Huston has a mind like a rapier. He cuts the opposition into small pieces, holds each one up for the inspection of the audience, then tosses it aside disdainfully. Muehl has a mind like a bludgeon. He clubs his opponent's case into an unrecognizable pulp and hurls the bloody corpse at your feet.

But Muehl said he opposed "semantic battering rams" in arguing about major social issues—politics, racism, sexism, and classism. He said they destroy rational discourse and cause "the tone of community discourse . . . [to go] into a downward spiral. So let's have no more of this rhetorical hooliganism!"

10. Threats can be made bluntly or quite gently, but they should always be taken seriously. Consider the experience of the man who was walking along a dimly lit street in a large city. Suddenly, a menacing figure emerged from a little alley and said, "Please stop."

The man who was walking did stop and, feeling very nervous, asked, "What do you want?"

The man in the alley gently responded: "I wish you would be so kind as to help me. I'm a poor, unfortunate fellow, hungry and out of work. All I have in the world is this gun."

11. One morning, Stanfield came to work with a black eye, a swollen lip, and looking rather fragile. The boss asked him, "What in heaven's name happened, Stanfield?"

He replied, "I was talking when I should've been listening."

12. A fellow's car broke down on a deserted big-city street late one night. He got his flashlight and opened the hood to see what was wrong. As he was looking at the motor, he felt the car jiggling and realized someone was jacking it up in the back.

"Hey, what are you doing?" the fellow asked.

"Don't worry, man. Cool it! You're taking the battery, and I'm taking the tires."

13. A woman boarding a New York bus apologetically explained to the driver that she had forgotten her Senior Citizen pass.

"I'm sorry, ma'am," said the driver, "but you'll have to pay full fare."

The woman got very angry and exploded with "You go hell!"

A male voice was heard from the back of the bus: "Lady, is it OK if he lets me off at 59th Street first?"

14. In 1946, the U.S.A. began twelve years of nuclear-bomb testing on Bikini, a remote atoll in the Pacific. A vast number of crates of material had to be loaded on ships to provide for the tests. Although the crates were marked "Fragile" and "Delicate Instruments," the sailors were loading them very roughly. One of the scientists supervising the operation managed to change all that by calling to another scientist, "I really don't know which crate the bomb is in."

15. P. G. Wodehouse (1881-1975) depicted characters who were tremendously impressed, even terrified, by aunts. He writes about "Aunt calling to Aunt, like mastodons bellowing across primeval swamps." And even more impressive than aunts' voices were their eyes:

"She gave him a glance that would have roused pique in a slug."

"She had an eye that could open an oyster at twenty paces."

By the way, that sort of glance and eye can be very useful for a teacher who has unruly pupils in her class.

16. A woman in a battered car was heading rapidly for a parking space when a man tried to turn into the same space. She leaned out her window and shouted, "Are you going to fight me for that space?"

Hitting the brakes, the man yelled back, "No, ma'am. You look like a winner to me."

17. A perceived threat is often more a matter of demeanor than of action. During his first year at Cambridge University in England, a student there was giving his father a tour of the place. As they made the rounds, a very formidable looking woman strode by, gave a curt nod, and went on.

"Who's that?" asked the father, very impressed.

"That's Miss Ekhart," replied the student. "She's the mistress of Ridsley Hall."

The father looked amazed and asked, "Who is Ridsley Hall?"

18. Mr. Loomis was very annoyed when a neighbor phoned at 3 a.m., huffed angrily, "Your dog is barking so loudly that I can't sleep," and then hung up before Loomis could reply.

But he had an idea for revenge. At 3 a.m. the next night he called the neighbor, said, "This is Loomis. I don't have a dog," and hung up.

19. If you fly as much as I do, both on business and for pleasure, you know that when the plane taxis up to the airport gate, you are instructed not to unbuckle your seatbelts or stand in the aisle until the seatbelt sign goes off.

At the end of one trip a flight attendant's pleasant voice announced over the public address system: "If you get up before the seatbelt sign goes off, we'll shoot your baggage out the rear of the plane."

And I'm told that another attendant on a different flight said, "The captain will park our plane at Gate 76 in about three minutes. I've seen the captain's car, so I strongly suggest you remain seated."

Pleasures and Pleasantries

So enough about threats and unpleasantness, humorous though they may be. How about human behavior that is the opposite of threatening?

20. In 1983, Kathleen Keating wrote an excellent work, *The Hug Therapy Book* (Comcare Publications, 1983). So what is good about hugging? Here are three brief Keating paragraphs that give the essence:

Hugging is healthy: It helps the body's immunity system. It keeps you healthier, it cures depression, it reduces stress, it induces sleep, it's invigorating, it's rejuvenating, it has no unpleasant side effects, and hugging is nothing less than a miracle drug.

Hugging is all natural: It is organic, naturally sweet, has no pesticides, no preservatives, no artificial ingredients, and is 100 percent wholesome.

Hugging is practically perfect: There are no movable parts, no batteries to wear out, no periodic checkups, low energy consumption, high energy yield, inflation-proof, non-fattening, no monthly payments, no insurance requirements, theft-proof, non-taxable, non-polluting and, of course, fully returnable.

21. A modest, unspectacular woman was one of the best-liked people in her small-town community. Someone once asked her, "How do you do it? How do you keep so many friends?"

"Well, sir, I follow one simple rule," she replied. "I'm always very careful to taste my words before I let them pass my teeth."

22. One of the most wonderful concepts in Judaism is that of the *mitzvah*—a good and Godly act done without any expectation of, or desire for, getting credit. I doubt if Charles Lamb (1775-1834), the famous English essayist, knew the term *mitzvah*, but he did know about doing good—with a twist. He wrote: "The greatest pleasure I know is to do a good act by stealth, and to have it found out by accident."

So up with *mitzvath* (plural) and down with holier-than-thouness and show-off do-gooders!

23. There is, at least according to the British, no more satisfactory beverage than tea. Statesman William E. Gladstone (1809-1898), who was Prime Minister during four periods between 1868 and 1894, made this remark about tea: "If you are cold, tea will warm you; if you are heated, it will cool you; if you are depressed, it will cheer you; if you are excited, it will calm you."

Sounds like a pretty good addiction.

24. James Thurber (1894-1961), the American humorist and famous contributor to *The New Yorker,* said this about humor: "By definition, humor is gentle. The savage, the cruel, the harsh would fall under the heading of wit and/or satire, as the lawyers say. Now, my definitions are these: The wit makes fun of other persons; the satirist makes fun of the world; the humorist makes fun of himself, but in so doing, he identifies himself with people—that is, people everywhere, not for the purpose of taking them apart, but simply revealing their true nature."

Dorothy Parker (1893-1967) would probably have only partially agreed, for she said: "Wit has truth in it; wisecracking is simply calisthenics with words."

Sometimes a person needs to find a gentle way to suggest a reform in behavior.

25. Mrs. Sanville after reading her husband's shopping list—cheese, coffee, salt, doughnuts, pork chops, cigarettes, bacon, butter, sugar, whiskey, gin—archly inquired, "Darling, is this a shopping list or a suicide note?"

26. Some people get a gentle, fond pleasure out of "doing evil." For instance, my mother, Edith Warner Johnson (1889-1974), was a strong believer in the right, and joy, of kids to be naughty—naughty, not bad! She also believed in swearing, not at people, but in general: "Damn you!"—no. "Damn!"—OK. "Go to hell!"—no. "Hell!"—OK.

She loved to play golf but was a terrible player. Once she was playing with one of her many nieces, Peggy, who noticed that after each hole she carefully wrote on her scorecard. That day her score was about

125. As she was collecting her things, she put down the scorecard, and Peggy glanced at it. Beside each hole was written, "Damn!", "Hell!", "God!", "Blast!", "Damn!", etc.

"But, she never swore out loud," Peggy told me. "She wanted to be sure not to corrupt her niece."

Hot damn!

27. If you are lazy but very much enjoy fresh garden produce, there's a solution. Live next door to a vegetable garden and cultivate your neighbor.

28. In 1989-1990, the Central Park jogger case was, rightfully, big news, and what more terrible form of irresponsible, to-hell-with-it human behavior could there be than "wilding." I'm ashamed to say that in major U.S. cities there were T-shirts being sold blatantly displaying the motto: Let's Go Wilding. Well, I've been a regular jogger—not a runner—since 1968. Often I jog along the streets of Germantown and Mt. Airy (parts of Philadelphia).

What has impressed me most is how friendly people are when I pass by. I'm white; the population I jog among, in cars and out, is largely black. Almost always, when I come to a crossing with a four-way stop sign, the cars will stop and motion me to go first. People open their windows and yell, "Love it, Pop!"; "That's the way, Dude!"; or "Man, don't sweat to death. It's hot!" Little kids wait and say "Hi!"; toddlers say "Bye-bye!"; and almost everybody waves.

Who says it's a cruel, dangerous, evil world?!

(When I jogged in Calcutta, India, people would ask, "Why you are running?"; and in England men would say, "I could do with a bit o' that meself!")

Perspectives on Our Frailties, Foibles, and Problems

29. A person unknown to me, Helen Nielson, is reported to have said (and I agree with her): "Humility is like underwear—essential, but indecent if it shows."

A good example of this adage is the story about the Quaker kid, long ago, who boasted to a friend of his, "My father is humbler than thy father."

30. A British friend, whom I had asked to send me some humorous stories for *A Treasury of Humor,* wrote back: "Someone suggested that I should make a New Year's resolution to stop being lazy. I gave the idea some thought and finally decided against it because I couldn't be bothered. Maybe I'll give it up for Lent instead."

31. Mark Twain (1835-1910) knew what sort of people he liked and, I suppose, was not very religious. When a friend asked him where he thought he would be spending the afterlife, he replied, "Heaven for the climate, Hell for the company."

32. Sometimes, when we have a serious conversation with people on an important subject, they seem to think very logically and yet come out with conclusions that are obviously in error. In such cases, it is useful to remember what the American inventor and engineer Charles Franklin Kettering (1876-1958) said: "Logic is an organized method of going wrong with confidence."

33. One summer evening Thomas Edison (1847-1931) returned home from work. His wife said, "You've worked too long without a rest. You must take a vacation."

"But where will I go?" he asked.

"Decide where you'd rather be than anywhere else on earth and go there," she answered.

"Very well," promised Mr. Edison. "I will go tomorrow."

The next morning he went to his laboratory.

34. James Burrill Angell (1829-1916) was president of the University of Michigan from 1871 to 1909—35 years! One day, toward the end of his tenure, Angell was asked, "What is the secret of your success?" Angell replied, "Grow antennae, not horns."

This is pretty good advice for anyone in charge of a complex institution, whether educational, political, or commercial. However, President Dwight Eisenhower (1890-1969) had a different theory. When asked about leadership, he laid a small piece of string on his desk and said, "Look, if I try to push it, I get nowhere, but if I pull it, I take it anywhere I want."

35. A wise old man, when commenting on an acquaintance who never talked about anything but himself, said of the acquaintance: "He's a man who worships the vertical pronoun." [I]

Bending the Rules

36. Bill Muehl (1919-   ), whom we've already read about, is a recently retired teacher of preaching at the Yale Divinity School and a good friend of mine during summers at Randolph, N.H., a town full of preachers. In November 1980, he wrote a column for *Reflections*, a journal of the Yale Divinity School, titled "Freedom Football." Muehl writes:

Once upon a time there was a town filled with people who loved football. On crisp Saturday afternoons in autumn everyone who was not bedridden or in jail would go to the municipal stadium to watch two local teams battle one another on a well-turfed gridiron . . . .

One bright October afternoon, however, during the halftime festivities a very strange thing happened. A figure dressed in a clown suit ran onto the field carrying a bullhorn.

"Ladies and gentlemen," he shouted, "it seems to me that we are playing this game in a highly legalistic fashion. Our whole emphasis is upon rules and regulations rather than freedom and possibility. Why should we require one side to advance the ball exactly ten yards in order to keep possession of it? We ought to be more relaxed about the matter and let the team that appreciates it keep the ball, as long as it demonstrates a good spirit. And should it be necessary for the ball to be carried into the end zone for a score? I propose that we give points for imaginative choreography

24 HUMOROUS STORIES ABOUT THE HUMAN CONDITION

in the backfield and a cheerful demeanor in the line."

Most of the spectators were nonplussed by these proposals. But they loved football. And anything that promised to improve the game commended itself to them. They feared, also, to seem too rigid, lest their neighbors suspect them of being conservatives. So they called out approval of what the man in the clown suit suggested. Some of them even got far enough into the spirit of things to start making additional proposals of their own.

"Why are the same players on the same side throughout the game? Let's rotate the linemen after each play," cried one.

"A great idea," shouted another. "But is there any reason why only twenty-two men are having all the fun, while the rest of us just sit and watch? I say we should all get really *involved* and feel more *relevant* to the fray."

Upon hearing these words the crowd rose from its seats and clambered over the barrier onto the field. Spare balls were brought out from the locker rooms and tossed into the milling throng. A glorious melee broke out. People ran now one way and then another, helping both teams with splendid impartiality. The whole scene was one of glorious freedom and enthusiastic participation.

When the setting sun heralded the onset of evening (the time-keepers had been trampled to death by the throng) and a faint chill crept into the air, the man in the clown suit announced that the game had ended. All the people gathered in a great circle around the edges of the field, held hands and sang "Amazing Grace."

On their way home from the stadium everyone agreed that it had certainly been a wonderful afternoon and that their favorite sport had undergone a marvelous liberation. But no one ever went out to the field again. That was the last football game.

So Bill Muehl attacks, metaphorically, the moral and social flabbiness of our society, even while at the same time criticizing our rigidity and violence.

Is our society rigid and violent? Or do we behave merely selfishly—according to the rules?

37. A man was overheard saying to his friend in the coffee shop of a U.S. government office: "Gosh, I'd better get back to the office or I'll be late for quitting time!"

A similar story, out of government, is about the person who asked, "I wonder if there is life after death?"

Her friend replied, "There sure is. You should see what happens at our office at five o'clock!"

Human, All Too Human

And we close this chapter on our behavior and personal relationships with a miscellany of humorous stories about both.

38. At a fancy party in Washington around the turn of the century, the host was passing around cocktails. He offered one to a woman and then suddenly said, "Oh, no. I shouldn't offer you a drink. I'd forgotten that you're president of the Anti-Saloon League."

The woman replied, "No, that's quite all right. I'd be glad to have a cocktail. You see, I'm not the president of the Anti-Saloon League; I'm president of the Anti-Vice League."

"Oh, yes," said the man. "Well, I knew there was *something* I shouldn't offer you!"

39. There was a man riding on a train with a banana stuffed in each ear. Eventually, curiosity overcame the politeness of a fellow-passenger. "Excuse me," he said, "but why have you got those bananas stuffed in your ears?"

"You'll have to speak louder, sir," answered the man. "I've got bananas stuffed in my ears."

40. A little girl named Georgia tended to have very definite opinions and to express them vigorously. Her Uncle Greg, noticing this, commented, "Georgia, fools are certain; wise men hesitate."

"Are you sure about that, Uncle Greg?" asked Georgia.

"Yes, my girl, I'm certain of it."

41. A police officer flashed his lights, blew his siren, and made a woman pull over to the side of the road.

She rolled down her window and said, "Oh, Officer, was I driving too fast?"

"Not at all, madam," replied the officer. "You were flying too low."

42. A husband and wife were discussing the day's events. The wife said, "That new cleaning lady must have stolen two of our new towels."

"Well, some people are like that," replied the husband. "By the way, which towels were they?"

"Oh, the ones we brought back from that nice big motel in Kansas City," said the wife.

43. These days, perhaps a minor misfortune is that feminism has resulted in a reduction of gallantry. An example of this is the woman who was struggling out of the supermarket with a lot of heavy bags. A man observed her and said, "Madam, may I carry your bags to your car? It would give me great pleasure."

"Thank God," she replied, "a male chauvinist pig!"

44. George Bernard Shaw (1856-1950) was a tall, very thin man. An acquaintance, G.K. Chesterton (1874-1936), a prolific English writer, noted for his rotundity, said to Shaw, "To look at you, one would think there was a famine in England."

Shaw replied, "Chesterton, to look at you one would think you were the cause of it."

45. A French priest was traveling by train to Italy. On the way, he struck up an acquaintance with some Italians who had bought a lovely, expensive "ladies' kit" in France and wanted to get it through customs duty-free. They asked the priest if he could help and were surprised when he readily agreed, even though he said he always told the truth. So the priest put the purchase under his cassock.

When the priest went through customs, he declared, "Above my belt I have a pure and truthful heart. Below my belt I have an unused ladies' kit."

46. When you can get away with less, why make a great effort? Two maids were discussing their employers.

Maid One: "The woman I work for says I should always warm the plates for her dinner guests. It's a lot of work."

Maid Two: "Oh, I know the solution for that one. Me, I just warm the hostess's plate. It's a lot less work, and she never knows the difference."

47. Sometimes even people in love can misinterpret a question. (And so can long-married couples!) A young man and woman who were romantically involved were driving silently along a beautiful woodland road at dusk. The young lady said softly, "Mike dear, can you drive with one hand?"

"Oh, yes, darling," he replied, with excitement in his voice.

"Well, dear," she said less softly, "then you'd better wipe your nose."

48. We hear much of the value of strong motivation and of constant persistence. However, W. C. Fields (1880–1946), the famous rasping, bulbous-nosed actor, countered this idea when he said, "If at first you don't succeed, try, try again. Then quit. No use being a damn fool about it."

And that leads us into the subject of chapter 2. After all, isn't motivation, despite its "damn fool" aspects, a major element of education? I believe it is (and research shows it), as I demonstrate in my non-humorous book *Raising Children to Achieve: A Guide for Motivating Success in School and Life,* published by Walker Publishers, New York, N.Y. (phone to order: 212-265-3632). Who says I'm not motivated!

2

Education, Teachers, and Teaching

The Teaching Profession: Various Perspectives

If teachers wonder whether they are appreciated or not, the following may help.

> **49.** The profession of teaching should be strongly recommended. A teacher is in a company that includes teachers as ancient as Socrates (469–399 B.C.), as revolutionary as Rousseau (1712–1778), and as modern as Margaret Mead (1901–1978). Anyone worrying about law, medicine, and politics should remember that wonderful scene in *A Man for All Seasons* by the British playwright Robert Bolt (1924–   ), when Sir Thomas More (Saint Thomas More, 1478–1535) asks Richard Rich, who is looking for a post at court, "Why don't you teach?" Rich replies rather plaintively, "But who would know?"
>
> More responds, "You, your students, your friends, God: not a bad public."

A more sobering view of the profession is this example of youthful realism.

> **50.** Some ten-year-olds in Plymouth Council School, England, were told to write an essay on "What I Hope to Be When I Grow Up." One girl began her essay thus: "I have great hopes of becoming a film star, but as I have neither good looks nor sex appeal, I suppose I shall have to be just a teacher."

51. In a good school, students are well-motivated, and so are teachers. When I was doing consulting work for some schools in Maryland, teachers told me about a school conference room that was next to the superintendent's office in one district. The superintendent, being a conscientious man who believed in effective motivation, had all the student art work removed from the room and replaced with charts showing the test scores for each school. The teachers referred to the place as "The Applied Anxiety Room."

52. Sometimes teachers, and even principals, get a little weary of their jobs, including both the material they teach and the pupils who are supposed to be learning. One Friday afternoon in the faculty room a teacher was heard to sigh and then to say to her colleagues, "You know what education is? It's casting false pearls before real swine."*

The Virtues of Self-Examination

One of the important ways to have children do well in school is to ask them to examine themselves.

53. Betty Cunningham, an ingenious teacher of second grade at Germantown Friends School in Philadelphia, sometimes asks her pupils to write brief, honest self-reports. Here is a sampling of some she gave me when she knew I was working on a book:

- I need to work on listening to other people. I have too loud a voice.
- My geometry is good but it still needs to improve because my lines and circles are still wiggly.
- Now I work more and talk less.

---

*This remark is based on a passage from Jesus's Sermon on the Mount, Matthew 7:6—"Give not that which is holy unto the dogs, neither cast ye your pearls before swine, lest they trample them under their feet, and turn again and rend you."

- My manners are excellent. I need a little more sense of humor. I guess I am a little too serious.
- I am always losing something in my desk.
- I need to stop worrying about silly things.
- I should think more in math.
- I am not very good in geometry because I cannot keep the compass point on the paper.
- Mrs. Cunningham makes me work very hard but I don't care. I want to know a lot.

Buckle Down!

I guess we all "want to know a lot," but are we ready to practice, in reality, or are we just pretending?

54. Sinclair Lewis (1885-1951), the author of *Main Street*, *Babbit*, *It Can't Happen Here*, and many other novels about America, was invited to give a lecture to college students who wanted to go into literature. He went to the lecturn, got out his notes, looked at the group and asked, "How many of you really intend to be writers?"

All the students raised their hands.

"In that case," said Lewis, "go home and write."

With that, he folded up his notes and left the room.

55. It's tough to be a scholar, at least for some (but not for Einstein [see story 267] or Edison [see story 33]. This is vividly described by Robert Burton (1577-1640), the clergyman and scholar who wrote in his *Anatomy of Melancholy* (1621):

Hard students are commonly troubled with gowts, catarrhs, rheums, cachexia, bradypepsia, bad eyes, stone, and collick, crudities, oppilations, vertigo, winds, consummations, and all such diseases as come by over-much sitting: they are most part lean, dry, ill-coloured . . . and all through immoderate pains and extraordinary studies. If you will not believe the truth of this, look upon great Tostatus and Thomas Aquinas' works; and tell me whether those men took pains.

Special Exception

Sometimes, even in the best schools, unexpected problems come up.

56. Horace Dutton Taft was headmaster of the Taft School in Watertown, Connecticut. He was a strict disciplinarian but also had a great sense of humor. At Taft, there was one absolute rule: that no boy could take an unscheduled vacation.

But a problem arose. Taft's nephew, the son of his brother William Howard Taft (1857-1930), asked to be excused to attend his father's inauguration as President of the United States. Horace Taft pondered. After all, rules are rules and must be obeyed. So he had a new rule passed, which is still, I understand, a part of the school's legal code. It reads: "Any boy whose father is elected to the Presidency of the United States shall be permitted to attend the inauguration ceremonies."

Left-Handed Compliment

57. It's tough to be a principal of a school. When the PTA held a celebration of the principal's twentieth anniversary as school head, the cake was inscribed: "Twenty years of stumbling—*in the right direction.*"

May we all "stumble in the right direction"! Otherwise, we become dictators. Dictators never stumble; they just crash.

Circumlocutions, Bad Grammar, and Hyperbole

58. Sometimes teachers have a hard time calling a spade a spade, or they use long words to do it. Take for example the teacher who gave her class a writing assignment and then went out into the hall to speak to a colleague. Peering back into the classroom, she noticed that all of the students were busy except for Gary. He was looking at the ceiling, doodling, tapping his fingers—everything except the assigned work. She turned to her fellow teacher and pointed to the boy: "Gary has an attention-deficit disorder."

59. Grammar can be a pretty dull subject, and sometimes it is defeated by logic, especially when there's too much routine repetition. An example is when little Don told his fourth-grade teacher, Mrs. Locke, "I ain't got no pencil."

Mrs. Locke leapt right in: "It's 'I *don't have* a pencil'; 'We don't have any pencils'; 'They don't have any pencils.' Is that clear?"

"No, Mrs. Locke, I don't get it," said Don. "What happened to all them pencils?"

Now we can go nearer the utlimate heights of education *and* the depths of immodesty.

60. Everyone knows about the benign rivalry between Harvard and Yale (alphabetical order: I'm a red-blooded Harvard man—no blue blood in me!). Well, many people, world-wide, would like to get a job at Harvard. According to his article "Deaning," in *Harvard Magazine*, Dean Henry Rosovky received the following job application from Algeria:

Dear Sir:

I have the honor to ask you to consider me for the post of professor in a suitable faculty.

I have nine Ph.D.'s. I have studied at Cambridge University. I have spent eighty years in the United States. I have known many American students. I have worked as a neurologist in many psychiatric hospitals of your country. I have studied geophysics and many languages, including Egyptian, French, Dutch, English, Chinese, and Japanese.

To tell you more about myself, I was the friend of a number of American presidents (George Washington, Roosevelt,

Lincoln). I am a veteran of the Civil war. I have worked with Metro-Goldwyn Mayer. . . .

"At this point," writes Rossovsky, "I stopped reading and sent the application to my friend, the provost of Yale. Our sister institution is especially famous for its humanistic studies, and I had the feeling that the gentleman from Algeria would find New Haven a more congenial environment."

Testing Teachers (and Pulling Their Legs)

61. An admirable way to improve the teaching of professors is used at Harvard. It's called the "one-minute paper." The method is to end the class lecture one or two minutes early and require each student to answer two questions:

1. What is the main point you learned in class today?
2. What is the major unanswered question you leave class with today?

The papers are written anonymously for the professor to read after class.

62. Teachers, and not always at Harvard, get asked some difficult, even humbling, questions, but then so do their pupils. At the end of the day a third-grader raised his hand.
"Yes, Paul? But we've only got a couple of minutes."
"Mrs. McKoy, what did we learn in school today?"
"That's a strange question," commented Mrs. McKoy. "Why do you ask that?"
"Because," said Paul, "that's what they always ask me when I get home, and I'm not sure how to answer."

63. Who says that very bright people don't go to obscure colleges? In Cape May, New Jersey, is Sheltren College. Next to the door of one of the college's lecture rooms there is a coatrack with a sign reading: "These hooks are reserved for faculty members."

Underneath the sign, a student wrote: "May also be used to hang hats and coats."

64. A famous scholar was known for his powers of reasoning and his ability to think his way through any dilemma. Some of his disciples wondered how well his reason would function if he was a wee bit tipsy, so during a social gathering they got him to drink enough to make him so tipsy that he fell asleep. While he slept, they gently carried him to the cemetery, where they laid him on the grass. Then they hid behind the tombstones and waited to see what would happen when he opened his eyes and realized where he was.

What he said when he awoke was a triumph of reasoning: "If I am living, then what am I doing here? And if I am dead, why do I want to go to the bathroom?"

65. At a certain school, the ninth-grade teacher happened to know a famous zoologist and asked him if he'd like to talk to her science class. He said yes, and they agreed that the subject would be "Rats: Dangerous Animals."

The zoologist gave an excellent talk, with vivid slides, and when it was over, one ninth-grader, who'd been appointed to thank the distinguished visitor, said: "Oh, we're so grateful, Dr. Kelly. Why, we didn't even know what a rat really looked like until you came to speak to us."

Teaching Aids

To teach effectively, one must be sure that the instruction is put in terms that the learner can understand. Here's a prime example of good teaching in a home setting.

66. These days more and more fathers are learning how to care for babies, but sometimes it's not easy unless their wives can help them draw from their own experience. When her husband looked puzzled and frustrated by the task of putting on a diaper, his ingenious wife said, "OK, dear, it's pretty simple. The diaper is a baseball diamond. Bring second base to home plate and lay the baby between first and third. Now bring first, third, and home together; then pin. But be sure to dust home plate with a little talcum powder."

Practical illustrations are also useful.

67. A number of years ago (when prices were much lower than they are now), a boy came into the village grocery and said to the grocer, "Write down ten pounds of sugar at 35¢ a pound; four pounds of coffee at 57¢ a pound; three pounds of butter at $1.05 a pound; and two cakes of soap at 35¢ each."

"OK, I've got them down," said the grocer.

"So how much is the total?" asked the boy.

"It's $9.63," replied the grocer.

"Well," said the boy, "if I were to give you a $20 bill, how much change would I get?"

"$10.37," said the grocer. "But I'm quite busy; so if you just give me the money, I'll put it all in a bag for you."

"Oh, I don't want to buy anything," said the boy. "But thanks! That's our arithmetic lesson for tomorrow and I needed help."

The Peculiar Files of Biology Teachers

68. A biology teacher I know, who is also a homeroom teacher, told me of two amusing messages she received one year. The first was from a parent and read, "Please excuse Joe today. His chameleons are mating."

The other message was from the school secretary: "Notice to tenth grade: Two dozen fertilized eggs arrived this morning. Be prepared."

Getting the Message Across

69. The teacher explained to her fifth-grade arithmetic class, "In order to subtract, things have to be of the same *denomination*. For example, you couldn't take three pears from four peaches. Neither could you take eight horses from ten cats."

A bright girl eagerly raised her hand.

"Yes, Mary?" said the teacher. "What is it?"

"Well," said Mary, "I'm sure a farmer could take three quarts from two cows."

70. In science class, the teacher tried to impress the pupils with the speed of light. She said, "Isn't it extraordinary?! The sun is 93 million miles away from the earth. But its light travels to earth at 186,000 miles per second. So it only takes about 8 minutes to get here!"

A boy raised his hand.

"Yes, Zack?" said the teacher.

"Well, Mrs. Mellor," replied Zack. "It's not such a big thing. After all, it's downhill all the way."

Ingenious Strategems of Teachers and Students

71. Sometimes teachers need to be ingenious to get at the truth without seeming to attack students they suspect of lying: A shrewd high school teacher, Mr. Selby, confronted four of his students who didn't get to school until after lunch. "What happened?" he asked.

"Well, Mr. Selby," replied one boy, "we had a flat tire."

"I'm sorry to hear that," said Selby, "but you missed the test. Sit down right now at these desks well apart from each other."

The boys did so.

"OK," said Selby, "the first question is: Which tire was flat?"

72. A young girl, struggling to maintain a C average, asked her father, "Dad, can you sign your name with your eyes closed?"

"Well, I don't know, Honey," said Dad. "I've never tried. But why do you ask?"

With an earnest expression, she replied, "Pop, I want you to sign my report card."

73. Children, even when they are having difficulties, are pretty ingenious about getting around them. This is shown by the case of a kid who had a hard time pronouncing the letter r. His teacher gave him this sentence to practice on: "Robert gave Richard a rap in the ribs for roasting the rabbit so rare."

A week later, the teacher asked him to recite the sentence, and, with great confidence, he proclaimed: "Bob gave Dick a poke in the side for not cooking the bunny enough."

Lovable Smart Alecks

Sometimes, to the delight of good teachers or the annoyance of mediocre ones, pupils can display wit as well as obedience.

74. A rather proper teacher took over a new class in the middle of the year. She asked the class to tell her their names.

"Jule," replied the first boy.
"No, not Jule," she said. "It's Julius."
"OK," said Jule, "Julius."
Then she turned to the next boy. "And what's your name?"
"Billious," he replied.

75. Little Sarah came home from her first day in kindergarten. "How did it go?" asked her mom.

"Well, OK, I guess," Sarah said. "Some woman wanted to know how to spell *cat*, and I told her."

76. The Country School in Madison, Connecticut, is a fine little independent school that goes through grade 8. At the graduation ceremony, someone delightedly remembered this: "Ten years ago a little girl—you may notice her here—entered our pre-kindergarten. Usually alert even then, she was sitting near her teacher one day as they laughed loudly over a story. When the story was over, she approached her teacher with great seriousness: "I noticed you have a lot of fillings. Have you seen your dentist lately?'"

Now that's the kind of careful observation and spirit of helpfulness schools should develop in their kids!

The Sad But Laughable Side of American Education

77. The American journalist Harry Lewis Golden (1902-81) published *The Carolina Israelite*. He was an ingenious thinker about difficult social problems, including racial integration. During the fifties, he noticed that white people in North Carolina had no objection to standing up with black people, only to sitting down with them. Therefore, he developed Harry Golden's Plan for the Vertical Integration of the Schools. It was simple: You just take the chairs out of the schools and have the pupils stand behind their desks.

78. A totally objective scientific experiment is almost impossible to accomplish. Once experimenters have invested their time in collecting data, tabulating it, and testing out the theories which they hope to prove or disprove, it is extremely difficult to be objective. I have found this to be especially true in the field of education. Over the years, I have read reports of scores of experiments, and almost all of them show better ways to teach and to improve learning, discipline, etc., etc., *ad nauseam*. Hardly ever—perhaps *never*—does something not work. This is what a very wise old educational scientist had in mind when he stated: "All educational experiments are doomed to succeed."

79. Things are undoubtedly getting better in many of our schools today, but a few years ago (according to a file document I was shown), a teacher got fed up and decided to resign. Her principal asked her why, and she handed him this statement: "In our schools the teachers are afraid of the principals; the principals are afraid of the superintendents; the superintendents are afraid of the board; the board is afraid of the parents; the parents are afraid of the children. *And:* the children aren't afraid of anybody."

3

Signs of Life—I

One of my great pleasures over the years has been noting down the words or signs I have either seen myself or read about. A good sign is often a way to help—and to keep helping—people solve problems or to make problems easier to live with.

As you will see from the Table of Contents, there are four brief chapters in this book on signs, titled Signs of Life I through IV. Many signs, as you may have observed, convey tersely, and sometimes wisely and wittily, messages about human behavior. (Of course, some signs can be dull, obscure, long, and even incomprehensible.) Here, then, are some signs that are relevant to education.

> **80.** As I walked about the halls and classrooms of a school which I was visiting in my role as a consultant, I could see from some of the items posted on the bulletin boards that there was at least one wit in the school. Here are six pithy messages I noted:
>
> - A spoken word is not a sparrow. Once it flies out, you can't catch it.
>
> - A single fact will often spoil an interesting argument.
>
> - You're never too old to grow up.
>
> - Most problems precisely defined are already partially solved.
>
> - Good habits are as easy to form as bad ones.
>
> - Confidence is contagious.

81. And some more in other schools:

- Parent: A thing so simple even a child can operate it [obscurely placed in a school principal's office]
- You can't hold a good man down without staying down with him.—Booker T. Washington [in the hall of a large urban school]
- Jumping to conclusions is not half as good exercise as digging for facts. [in a Harvard lecture hall]
- At Harvard University, a new library was to be built, and a professor of philosophy was asked for a motto to engrave in stone in the front of the edifice. He chose: "Man is the measure of all things." (Protagoras, 490?-415? B.C.) Then the professor went on sabbatical, and when he returned he went to see how the motto looked. Here is what he read: "What is man that thou are mindful of him?" (Paul's Epistle to the Hebrews, 2, 6)
- We bus drivers are the only people with all of our problems behind us. [in a school bus garage]
- Silence, please. Remember, even a fish wouldn't get caught if it kept its mouth shut. [in a school library]

4

Language: What Words Can Do For and To Us

Out of the Mouth of Babes

82. A little girl came home from school looking rather out of sorts. Her mother asked her, "What's the matter, dear? Did something bad happen at school?"

"Well, I didn't like the teacher we had today, Mom," replied the child. "Mrs. Rinker was sick and so we had a prostitute teacher."

83. A kindergarten teacher was explaining to her youngsters some simple body facts. She pointed to her chest. "This is where your heart is," she said.

A boy raised his hand and said, "No! My heart is where I sit down."

"What do you mean?" asked the teacher.

"Well," answered the boy, "every time I do something good, my mommy pats me there and says, 'Bless your little heart.' "

84. Young children often invent very apt ways of saying things. A former student of mine thought that I as an English teacher would enjoy a question his three-and-a-half-year-old son had asked. It was time to go off to the day care center. The boy looked around and queried urgently, "Whobody's gonna fix my lunch?"

85. We Americans get so used to baseball that we often fail to see how difficult it is for youngsters, especially those who are just learning their basic English vocabulary, to make sense of it. (It's even worse for foreigners.)

A kid asked his dad, "Why do they call that thing a home plate? It doesn't look like a plate, and it's sure not at home." Then, after pondering some more, he said, "It's stupid. When they say the batter had a strike, it means he missed; he didn't hit anything."

"Well, Son, it's a special vocabulary," said Dad.

"Special? It sounds crazy to me. It's even bad grammar. My teacher wouldn't allow us to say, 'A batter flied out' instead of 'flew out.' And how can a ball be 'foul' at one time and 'fair' another. It's not fair!"

"Yeah, Son, when you're a little bit older . . . ."

"Wait a minute, Dad. I'm not finished. When a guy scores a run on a big hit, they say he hit a home run, but he didn't. He just goes around the diamond (whatever that is!) and ends up at home plate. When I have a home plate, I want food on it, or else, if I'm good, I wash it."

86. In the back country a mother, father, and their small son Greg were moving into a very modest house. The boy asked, "Dad, how many doors will our new house have?"

The father replied jokingly, "Three, Greg—a front door, a back door, and a cuspidor."

A little while later Greg was heard explaining to a friend, "Gee, our new house has three doors—a front door, a back door, and a door for swearing."

The Pitfalls and Pratfalls of English

Spelling, grammar, and punctuation are important parts of language, and they can be fun, bothersome, or just useful. Let's look at some fun about a bother.

87. A word-loving, irreverent friend of mine sent me this. I hope it will encourage you to split when it makes clear sense to do so!

SPLITTING THE INFINITIVE

One of the most closely guarded secrets of the era can now be told, how an anonymous group of grammarians, working in secrecy in a remote section of the country, have finally succeeded in splitting the infinitive.

The so-called "BRONX PROJECT" got under way in 1943, with the installation of a huge infinitron specially constructed for the job by Cal. Tech. philologists. Though the exact details are still withheld for reasons of security, it is possible to describe the general process.

From a stockpile of fissionable gerunds, encased in leaden clichés to prevent radioactivity, a suitable subject is withdrawn and placed in the INFINITRON together with a small amount of syntax. All this material must be handled with great care, as the slightest slip may lead to a painful solecism. Once inside the apparatus, the gerund is whirled about at a great speed, meanwhile being bombarded by small particles. A man with a Gender Counter stands always ready to warn the others if the Alpha-Betical rays are released in such high quantities as to render the scientists neuter.

The effect of the bombardment is to dissociate the whirling parts of speech from one another until at length an infinitive splits off from its gerund and is ejected from the machine. It is picked up gingerly with a pair of hanging clauses and plunged in a bath of pleonasm. When it cools, it is ready for use.

The question is often asked: Can other countries split the infinitive? I think we can safely answer "No." Though it is true that Russia, for one, is known to have large supplies of thesaurus hidden away behind the Plural Mountains, it is doubtful if the Russians have the scientific technique. They have the infinitive but not the know-how.

And that is something on which to congratulate our own brave pioneers in the field of grammatical research. Once it was thought that the infinitive could not be split—at least, not without terrible repercussions. We have shown that it is quite possible, given the necessary skill and courage, to unquestionably and without a shadow of a doubt accomplish this modern miracle.

LANGUAGE: WHAT WORDS CAN DO FOR AND TO US

88. George Bernard Shaw (1856-1950) was greatly in favor of simplifying English spelling. To make his point, he maintained that the word *fish* should be spelled *ghoti*. How come? Well, *gh* as in tough or cough; *o* as in women; and *ti* as in sensation.

Shall we reform—or adjust to habit?

89. A puzzle given by a grammar teacher to some bright students challenged them to write a correct sentence using the word *had* at least ten times. The winner came up with this: "John, where James had had 'had had,' had had 'had.' 'Had had' had had a better effect on the teacher."

(A similar repetitive verbal truth is: "That that is, is; that that is not, is not; is not that it? It is.")

90. A professor of English with an interest in both punctuation and sociology, decided to test his students. He said, "All right, class, we have a few minutes. Please punctuate this sentence," and he wrote on the chalkboard: "Woman without her man is a savage."

Can you guess how the punctuation of the male students and the female students was different? Try it. Then look at the answer printed upside down at the bottom of this page. *

91. Examine this sentence carefully and tell what's wrong with it: "When it comes to English grammar, almost everybody has their own pet peeves."

Well, there are two things "wrong" with the sentence, and I bet that you, like me, missed the most important one the first time you looked at the sentence. The most provably wrong thing about the sentence is that it is false! In fact, a very small part of the population has a pet peeve about English grammar. Most people, as they say, "could care less."

So: don't let preoccupation with the agreement of pronouns and verbs, etc., blind you to larger truths.

---

*Males: Woman without her man is a savage.
Females: Woman! Without her, man is a savage.

92. Placing modifiers in the correct place is an important way to make your writing clear. Try placing the adverb *only* in every possible place before, in, or after the following sentence and see how many startlingly different meanings you get.

"Oscar hit Vera in the eye yesterday."

93. Sometimes in casual classroom talk, even teachers fail to say what they really mean. One day, during a writing period, a third-grade boy raised his hand and said, "I lost my eraser."

"That's no problem," said the teacher. "Use the little girl's behind."

Foreign Tongues and Tongue Twisters

Did you love Latin at school? Here are two delights about that language.

94. I admit that I had only two years of Latin in high school and found it very dull, despite an excellent teacher. It seemed to me that the Romans never talked about anything ordinary or made casual remarks such as: "Hi! How are things going?"; "What happened downtown yesterday?"; "Boy, do I feel punk today!"; etc. Latin seems to have been all about battles, maps, and the three parts of Gaul, or dull slogans or mottoes.

Once, to test a Latin enthusiast, I expressed my feelings about Latin and asked her, "How, for example, would the Romans have said, 'Caesar had to pee in the middle of the night'?"

She thought and thought and then said, "I'll tell you tomorrow." Tomorrow came; I asked her again; and she replied, "I've figured it out. '*Caesar in media nocte aquam fecit.*'" ("Caesar in the middle of the night made water.")

I'll admit there's one Latin phrase that I prefer to its English original. It was composed by Vannevar Bush (1890–1974), the famous electrical engineer and physicist, who was professor at the Massachusetts Institute of Technology and developed computers as well as the atomic bomb. When frustrated, he would say, "Illegitimus non carborundum," which, roughly translated, means, "Don't let the bastards grind you down."

95. A Latin teacher was trying out fountain pens in a stationery store. As the salesman watched, the teacher wrote "*Tempus Fugit*" ("Time flies.") a couple of times with each pen. He didn't seem quite satisfied, and the salesman said, "Well, here's the really finest pen we've got. Please try it, Mr. Fugit."

96. As you probably remember, Ferdinand the Bull was very gentle, and refused to run, jump, and butt. He just sat and smelled the flowers. Well, an unknown person, a speaker of Spanish, retold the story in the best English he could manage. The result is English as a Second Language (ESL) at its noblest:

FERDINAND, THE BULL

The mother of Ferdinand who was, by chance, a cow, asked from the latter on account of what thing he was not running and jumping. "It ought to be for a disgrace to you," she said, "not to jump and run." It was pleasing, however, to Ferdinand, to sit under a certain cork tree and to perceive the flowers by means of his nose. Ferdinand having being born three years while he was sitting in the same place, saw certain men approaching to himself, who, in truth, were coming in order that they might choose a bull who, because of great size and incredible boldness, might be able to fight with great bravery in the Arena in Madrid. Suddenly, however, Ferdinand having been bored through in respect to his rear by the small dart of a bee, jumping with great speed ran, now hither, now thither, and agitated the air by vast breathing.

The actual text as written by Munro Leaf in 1938 goes as follows:

Sometimes his mother, who was a cow . . . would say, "Why don't you run and play?" . . . But not Ferdinand—he still liked to sit quietly under the cork tree and smell the flowers.

One day five men came . . . to pick the biggest, fastest,

roughest bull to fight in the bull fights in Madrid. Ferdinand didn't look where he was sitting . . . and sat on a bumble bee . . . . The bee stung Ferdinand . . . . He jumped . . . and ran around puffing and snorting, butting and pawing.

As you may recall, Ferdinand was chosen, went to Madrid with great fanfare. But in the ring he saw the flowers in the lovely ladies' hair, and he sat down and smelled. So they took him home, where he is still "perceiving the flowers by means of his nose."

As we all know, people who speak the same language speak with different accents. There are even experts who can locate an American's native region within a few score miles just by listening to him or her speak. Here, however, is a story about a rather less delicate matter of accent.

97. Language is a matter of perspective, and the English tend to believe that they speak the correct version, known to some as "the King's English." This is illustrated by the comment of Prince Charles when he was in the U.S.A. and was shown a talking computer.

He listened to it work, was duly impressed, and then asked, "How do they teach it to speak with an American accent?"

98. Sometimes the accent we use when we speak affects the meaning of what we say. A wonderful example of this is quoted in Jonathan D. Spence's (1936-   ) superb book *The Search for Modern China* (Norton, 1990). Spence, a professor of history at Yale, illustrates how important intonation or accent is to the meaning of Chinese words by translating a Chinese passage in two different "accents." In the "northern accent" of China, the passage reads:

Everything prospers. Heaven is protective. People are heroes. The place is famous.

But in the Chinese "southern accent" of Canton (Guangzhou), a major marketplace for foreign trade and investment, the same passage reads:

Everything disintegrates. Heaven explodes. People are extinct. The place is bare.

So watch your accent!

Gobbledegook

One of the most delightful and humorous aspects of language is the way people mess it up unintentionally. There are mixed and super-mixed metaphors. There's *gobbledegook* (a word first used in 1944), much of it in government, some in business, and some even in careful publications.

>**99.** Recently the *Wall Street Journal,* a usually lucid paper, published the following sentence. If you can understand it, perhaps you'll make a million!

Whether increasing after-tax return to saving in general increases saving, whether increasing the after-tax return to a particular kind of saving increases saving in total, whether increasing the after-tax return to this particular kind of saving is more effective in increasing saving than is increasing the after-tax return to other kinds of saving or to saving in total—all are unanswered questions.

100. Even the most literate and thoughtful people can confuse their readers. Jerry Van Voorhis is a top-notch headmaster of Chatham Hall, an excellent small college-prep school in Chatham, Virginia. A short time ago in the school's alumnae magazine Van Voorhis wrote:

We are coming to understand in America again that community is a sum that is greater than the parts. The idea, as I say, most crippling to public and private schools is the opposite: namely, that community equals the sum of the parts, or what the parts say the sum is, thus what the parts are; and, therefore, should the parts not be in agreement, the parts at the expense of the sum, and even the other parts.

101. A competent, devoted doctor, who was always careful but *very* busy, sometimes let her language get a little bit loose. Once, when asked about a certain patient, she said, "Well, I should tell you that I have so many pots burning right now that I'm almost overwhelmed [at least she didn't say "whelmed over"!], but *please* be assured that we're watching the patient with a fine-toothed comb."

102. Governments—perhaps especially that of the U.S.A.—use fancy words to describe ordinary things. "Revenue enhancement" means a tax increase; that's obvious. But government and contractors (especially the military) can spend and receive more of our tax dollars by using terms like these:

- portable, hand-held communications inscriber
- hexiform rotatable surface compression unit
- manually-powered fastener-driving impact device

I think, but I'm not sure, these refer to pen or pencil, nut, and hammer.

103. Our local state representative, a fine man who shall here be nameless, appeared before a neighborhood group to talk about the insurance problems in the Commonwealth of Pennsylvania. I took some notes on his exact words. Here are three choice bits:

"We've got to go back to the drawing board and get a new game plan."

"They must loan us some dollars so we can get off the ground."

"With insurance the way it is, we're living on pins and needles."

104. Do you feel secure? If not, perhaps you should follow the suggestions of a man whose words were reported in the *Albany Times Union*, Albany, N.Y.:

But a fellow user pushing for stricter security counters: "Perhaps I am flogging a straw herring in midstream, but in the light of what is known about the ubiquity of security vulnerabilities, it seems vastly too dangerous for university folks to run with their heads in the sand."

LANGUAGE: WHAT WORDS CAN DO FOR AND TO US

105. There can be some pretty tough problems in the world, no doubt about it. But their difficulty was dramatically described by a member of a meeting, as reported in the *Tallahassee Democrat* of Florida, thus: "But an audience member warned that the solution might not be politically easy. 'Instead of the tail wagging the dog,' he said, 'you got to grab the bull by the horns and throw it. Maybe it's only pie in the sky but it's really going to be a bullet-biting baby."

106. Radio station KYW in Philadelphia is an essential part of my life, telling its listeners, "You give us 22 minutes, and we'll give you the world." A few years ago, they used to speak about "innermitten showers," but now, on Accuweather, its "shower activity" or even "snow activity." I'm waiting for the day when they come up with "fog activity." Why not just say "It's going to rain"?

Several times, when the announcer was being extra-cautious, I've heard, "There's a possibility of a chance of rain." Well, maybe.

Malapropisms, Neologisms, and Acronyms

107. The policeman brought a man into court. The judge asked, "Officer, what's the charge against this man?"

"Bigotry, Your Honor," said the policeman. "He has three wives."

The judge looked at the policeman disdainfully. "That's not bigotry," he explained. "That's trigonometry."

108. Adlai Stevenson (1900-1965) gave a speech, and afterward an older lady, who was not very well educated, came up to shake his hand. She exclaimed, "Mr. Stevenson, your speech was simply superfluous!"

Stevenson modestly replied, "Thank you. Perhaps I'll have it published posthumously."

"Oh, Mr. Stevenson," said the lady, "do—the sooner the better."

Now here are some simply superfluous—oops! I mean superb—bits of language.

109. In my *A Treasury of Humor* (1989), one of the most popular items was a list of *malaprops** and also *boniprops*. *The New York Times* columnist William Safire coined this word for a malaprop that is especially *bon* (good) as a way of saying things. Here are a number of boniprops readers of my first humor book have sent me:

- I'd like to be an eardropper on the wall.
- I'm not going to put my neck out on a limb.
- The fellow is out to butter his own nest.
- My gutteral reaction is that it's not true.
- Rome wasn't burned in a day.
- He's cutting off his nose in spite of his face.
- As for our budget, the upshot of the bottom line is . . . .
- Our best is none too good. (Sign on a clothing store in Korea.)
- Her name slips my tongue.
- Studies show that sterility may be inherited.
- Well, let's get onto some brass tacks.
- Airline slogan: Fly with us and you'll never walk again.
- He was groveling at the bit.
- It's an ill wind that gathers no moss.
- I'm feeling swamped; I've got too many balls in the fire.

---

*The word comes from the name of Mrs. Malaprop, a character in *The Rivals*, by Richard Sheridan (1751-1816). She is a chronic, unintentionally humorous misuser of words. Her name comes from the French *mal à propos*, "out of place."

LANGUAGE: WHAT WORDS CAN DO FOR AND TO US   53

- We've got to stop beating around the mulberry bush.
- She beat me to the pinch.
- With him, it just goes in one head and out the other.
- She doesn't carry her end of the stick.
- That's the way the world bounces.
- Were they alive today our Founding Fathers would turn over in their graves if they saw how loosely interpreted the First Amendment has become.
- The sands of time are ticking away.
- Deep down, she's really very shallow.
- The boy was stabbed in the suburbs.
- Young boy: "If I'm noisy, they spank me; if I'm quiet they take my temperature."
- The parable about the multitude that loafs and fishes.
- That stupid archaeologist's career lies in ruins.
- Bacteria reproduce by multiplying and dividing.

(*Note:* My champion boniprop-sender is John C. Esty, Jr., recent President of the National Association of Independent Schools in Boston.)

110. Probably many of my readers are vaguely aware that the longest word in the English language is supposed to be pneumonoultramicroscopicsilicovolcanoconiosis,—45 letters long, 19 syllables. It is a disease of the lungs that miners often get.

But here's a nicer word, 61 letters long, 27 syllables: *papiliocartigeniusnegrescensalbaliniadropextremitatibusalarum*

If you were such a small black butterfly, wouldn't you love to have a name like that!

111. In 1983, my wife and I went out to dinner at a small restaurant near Harvard Square. In this advanced, progressive area, people are especially careful to avoid sexist language. However, we were surprised when the person in charge came to our table and said, "Good evening! Your waitroid will be with you in a moment."

112. As head of a committee, a woman objected to the title "Chair." "I'm not a chair," she said to her husband, "and, furthermore, I refuse to have anything to do with personhole covers in the streets."
"I understand, dear," said her husband.
"And," she went on, "if our committee fails to get a piece of work done I suppose people will blame me and say, 'The chair allowed the matter to fall between two stools.' "
(Note: Years ago, a bright seventh grade student of mine objected to the term *chairperson*. "It should be *chairperdaughter*," she asserted, with a twinkle.)

113. If you ever find yourself feeling too sappily patriotic, just remember that our national anthem spelled backward is Rennab Delgnaps-Rats.

114. A few years ago, the pejorative term "bliss ninny" was often used. It meant a person who seeks bliss and thinks infrequently—and usually lives in a nice climate. These people, it is said, frequented the University of Arizona (with branches in Fayetteville, Little Rock, Monticello, and Pine Bluff).
In the University of Colorado, with four branches, and the University of South Carolina, only one campus, they were known as "lotus eaters."

Most people, I find, think that there is only one *correct* way to speak and write English. They forget that language is a form of human behavior, and over the years it changes. That's why it's important to have an excellent modern dictionary at hand. (I recommend *Webster's Ninth New Collegiate Dictionary*.)

Here are some examples of new ways of using words, passages, or initials.

LANGUAGE: WHAT WORDS CAN DO FOR AND TO US 55

115. Some people develop their vocabularies to an unreasonable—even vain—extent. A woman said to the bus driver, "I want to be procrastinated at the next corner."

Said the driver, "You want to be what?"

The woman replied, "Are you ignorant? I looked in the dictionary, and I discovered that *procrastinate* means put off. So, sir, procrastinate me at Chelten Avenue."

116. Both the First Congregational Church of Portland, Oregon, and The Zion Evangelical Congregational Church of Mohnton, Pennsylvania, published this version of the Twenty-third Psalm.

The 1989th Psalm

Recreation is my shepherd;
I shall not stay home.
It maketh me to lie down in a sleeping bag;
It leadeth me down the interstate each weekend.
It restoreth my suntan.
It leadeth me to state parks for comfort's sake.

Even though I stray on the Lord's Day,
I will fear no reprimand, for I am relaxed;
My rod and my reel they comfort me.

I anoint my skin with oil;
My gas tank runneth dry.
Surely my trailer shall follow me
    all the weekends of the summer,
And I shall return to the House of the Lord this fall.
But by then it will be hunting season,
And that's another Psalm.

117. My wife and I are on various committees in our neighborhood to help get jobs done and improve local life. Occasionally, a notice will go out saying something like this: "The Community Outreach committee will meet on Thursday, July 11, chez Johnson."

Well, believe it or not, the other day we received an appeal for money, and it was addressed to Mr. and Mrs. Chez Johnson.

118. Closely related to the above story is one that really happened to Professor Guy Mermier, a Frenchman who teaches at the University of Michigan. He and his wife, for fun, have a sign outside the door reading CHIEN MECHANT (French for BAD DOG). Recently, a person came to the door and addressed Mrs. Mermier thus, "Hello, Mrs. Mechant."

119. As I have suggested elsewhere in this book, acronyms are fun, and it's a form of intelligence to make them up. But perhaps, given the state of behavior of young people (probably no worse than it ever was—but anyway!), this is the ultimate example: ACRONYM — Action Committee to Reform Our Nation's Youth Morals.

Want to join?

120. Acronyms are delightful things: NOW (National Organization of Women); NASA (National Aeronautics and Space Administration); AA (Alcoholics Anonymous); SNAFU (Situation Normal, All Fouled Up); UN (United Nations); PTA (Parent-Teacher Association); or DAR (Daughters of the American Revolution). You can make up some of your own every day. A good example was when an elementary school principal (ESP—which also means extra-sensory perception) asked the teachers to suggest a name for a weekly staff newsletter. One of the suggestions was: FACULTY—Frantic Adults Chasing Unruly Little Tireless Youngsters.

Zap!

121. In 1990, Pennsylvania State Representative Ron Gamble suggested the following text as part of a State Senate bill requiring music labeling:

WARNING: May contain explicit lyrics descriptive of or advocating one or more of the following: Suicide, Sodomy, Incest, Bestiality, Sadomasochism, Adultery, Sexual activity in a violent context, Murder, Morbid Violence, Use of illegal drugs or alcohol. PARENTAL ADVISORY.

But way back in 1985, Frank Zappa (1940-   ), whose group, "The Mothers of Invention," became well-known (one of their songs was "Freak Out"), put his own label on records. It read:

> WARNING GUARANTEE: This album contains material which a truly free society would neither fear nor suppress.
>
> In some socially retarded areas, religious fanatics and ultra-conservative political organizations violate your First Amendment Rights by attempting to censor rock & roll albums. We feel that this is un-Constitutional and un-American.
>
> As an alternative to these government-supported programs (designed to keep you docile and ignorant), Barking Pumpkin is pleased to provide stimulating digital audio entertainment for those of you who have outgrown the ordinary.
>
> The language and concepts contained herein are GUARANTEED NOT TO CAUSE ETERNAL TORMENT IN THE PLACE WHERE THE GUY WITH THE HORNS AND POINTED STICK CONDUCTS HIS BUSINESS.
>
> This guarantee is as real as the threats of the video fundamentalists who use attacks on rock music in their attempt to transform America into a nation of check-mailing nincompoops (in the name of Jesus Christ). If there is a hell, its fires wait for them, not us.

Well, parents and even grandparents, which do you want, warnings or guarantees?

122. By now, given the fact that many couples "live" together without being married, most people are familiar with the phrase "significant other," although it hasn't made it into any dictionary that I am aware of. Another one, familiar but also not in the dictionary, is POSSLQ: People of Opposite Sex Sharing Living Quarters—or one could even try POSSSLQ: People of Same Sex Sharing Living Quarters.

However, I was surprised in the summer of 1990, when I asked someone how he knew an acquaintance of mine, to hear, "Oh, I'm his friend-in-law."

Perhaps you can say what it means. I was too embarrassed to ask.

Mind Your Tongue

123. Once Dr. Charles A. Beard (1874-1948), a professor of Columbia University, who helped found the New School for Social Research, spent a few days in a small town in Connecticut. It is said that the postmaster asked him, "What kind of a doctor are you?"

"I'm a doctor of philosophy," Beard replied.

"Oh, well, ah," said the postmaster, "I don't think we've ever had a case of that here."

124. You can't be too careful in the way you use language even when the intent is friendly, pleasant, and completely innocent. For example, Miss Landers, a kindergarten teacher, was traveling home in a city bus. She noticed a man across the aisle whom she thought she knew and she smiled very warmly at him. When he didn't respond, she realized she'd made a mistake and said, "Oh, excuse me. I mistook you for the father of two of my children."

125. The ancient Chinese were very wise about the danger of words. One of their proverbs is:

"Not the fastest horse can catch a word spoken in anger." And if you are a modern cybernetics lover (me, I'm cyberphobic—afraid of electronic devices), you might be interested in a new product I've heard about that helps you eat your words before they do any harm: a combination word processor and food processor.

And even God-loving preachers aren't immune to the dangers of words. A clergyman's son was watching his father write a sermon. The boy asked, "Dad, how do you know what to say?"

"God tells me," replied the preacher.

"Well, Dad," asked the boy, "then why do you cross so many things out?"

126. The Canadian Stephen Leacock (1869-1944) was an unusual combination—an economist and humorist. (Was it Leacock who commented that the science of economics was invented to make astrology look respectable?)

Two of his best volumes are *Literary Lapses* (1910) and *Winnowed Wisdom* (1926). He greatly enjoyed using language and making fun of it and its users. He wrote: "In Canada we have enough to do keeping up with the two spoken languages without trying to invent slang, so we just go right ahead and use English for literature, Scotch for sermons, and American for conversation."

Games and Conundrums

127. I've always had a fondness for palindromes: words, sentences, verses, or numbers that read the same forward as backward. The two classics are: "Madam, I'm Adam"; and (about Napoleon), "Able was I ere I saw Elba." But these two are nothing compared to an 82-letter example given to me by a passionately word-loving neighbor:

T. Eliot, top bard, notes putrid tang emanating. Is sad. Assign it a name: gnat dirt upset on drab pot toilet.

128. In some schools, upper-grade students are required to read the works of Chaucer (c. 1340–1400), the famous English poet, who wrote, among other works, *The Canterbury Tales* (17,000 lines long!). For centuries, he was unrecognized as a literary genius, and because of changes in the English language between 1400 and 1700, he was a difficult genius to understand.

A high school class was struggling with Chaucerian works, and the teacher asked, "Can anyone tell us whether Chaucer has been translated into other languages?"

A student, looking grim, raised her hand and said, "As far as I can tell, he hasn't even been translated into English yet."

Here are three of the easier Chaucerian passages:

"Hard is the herte that loveth nought/In May."

"Now welcome, somer, with thy sonne softe,
That hast this wintres weders overshake."

"Whan that Aprill with his shoures soote
The droghte of March hath perced to the roote."

129. The following letter, published in the *New York Times,* was written by Leonard Burkat, of Danbury, Connecticut, on February 5, 1990, under the heading "Of Gender, Sex, Grammar and All That":

In "Gender Messages" (letter, January 27), Michele S. Frank seeks to "show just how the arbitrary cultural construction of the gender line continues to shape the perception of women," but proves only that she does not understand how languages work. Many English-speaking women have taken ideological positions that have nothing to do with the difference between "gender" and "sex."

Gender is no more than a grammatical term. Sex is anatomical and physiological. French speakers know that the masculinity and femininity of words in their language are technicalities of grammar and have nothing to do with sex. "Soprano" can be masculine in their language, and the word for "bass" can be feminine.

In every language other than English with which I have the slightest acquaintance, nouns and their adjectives must be of the same gender, which leads to locutions mystifying to English speakers who imagine that barbaric foreigners are saying things like "her wife" and "his husband."

The failure of Americans to learn, understand and use languages other than English is a mark of greater arrogance than that often called "sexist" and is a great danger to our position in the world. Until this improves, let us all remember one simple fact of life: words have gender; people have sex.

Five Sharp-Tongued Celebrities

There are some well-known characters who used language in peculiar or ingenious ways. I give you five stories about five of them—all dead, but very much alive.

130. Harry Truman (1884–1972) was speaking at a Grange convention in Kansas City. His wife Bess was in the audience with a lady friend. Mr. Truman told the farmers the key to success was wrapped up in one word. "Manure," said Mr. Truman; "manure, manure, manure, manure, and more manure."

Mrs. Truman's friend whispered, "Listen, Bess, when are you ever going to get Harry to say fertilizer?"

Replied Mrs. Truman, "Good Lord, Marge, it's taken me thirty years to get him to say manure!"

131. Dorothy Parker (1893-1967), who wrote *Enough Rope, Death and Taxes,* and *Here Lies,* was listening to a crashing bore expounding his views in a solemn and ponderous manner. Finally, when he said, "I can't bear fools," Parker broke in with: "Oh? That's funny. Your mother could."

132. George Bernard Shaw (1856-1950) began his literary career as a music critic in London. One of his comments was, "Music is the brandy of the damned." Shaw was a stickler for good English. But sometimes he used bad English on purpose to make a point. After he had read a fellow-critic's analysis of Mozart's symphony in G minor, he wrote:

How succulent this is; and how full of Mesopotamian words like "the dominant of D minor!" I will now, ladies and gentlemen, give you my celebrated "analysis" of Hamlet's soliloquy on suicide, in the same scientific style. 'Shakespeare, dispensing with the customary exordium, announces his subject at once in the infinitive, in which mood it is presently repeated after a short connecting passage in which, brief as it is, we recognize the alternative and negative forms on which so much of the significance of repetition depends. Here we reach a colon; and a pointed pository phrase in which the accent falls decisively on the relative pronoun, brings us to the first full stop.'

... I want to know whether it is just that a literary critic should be forbidden to make his living in this way on pain of being interviewed by two doctors and a magistrate, and hauled off to Bedlam* forthwith; whilst the more a musical critic does it, the deeper the veneration he inspires.

133. One of the most famous lines in history is that spoken by Sir Henry Morton Stanley (1841-1904), the

---

*Bedlam: a London insane asylum.

British explorer who in 1871 was sent to find the famous medical missionary to Africa. When he did find him, he delivered the famous line, "Dr. Livingston, I presume?"

Many years later, some nut who enjoyed making up riddles, posed this one: What was the question that preceded the remark, "Dr. Livingston, I presume?"

Answer: "What is your full name, Dr. Presume?"

134. Oscar Fingal O'Flanertie Wills Wilde (1854–1900), the famous Irish writer and poet, had a wonderfully wry wit. He was extremely apt at expressing unexpected opposites:

- He's old enough to know worse.

- One can always be kind to people about whom one cares nothing.

- I do not approve of anything that tampers with natural ignorance.

- A gentleman is someone who is never unintentionally rude.

It is also reported that Wilde was in a restaurant where a string trio was making excruciating noises. Recognizing him, the maitre d' came over to ask if he had a request for the trio to play next. "Yes," answered Wilde, "dominoes."

Wit: Kind and Cruel

We close this chapter on language—but the *subject* of language is never closed—with nine examples of language used with special effectiveness, whether it be kind or cruel.

135. A gas station employee came into the office and said to his boss, "Abe, your doctor's here with a flat tire."

"Great!" said the boss. "Diagnose the trouble as a puncture wound resulting in a prolapsus of the perimetric membrane and prescribe plastic surgery to be fol-

LANGUAGE: WHAT WORDS CAN DO FOR AND TO US

lowed by the administration of violent flatulents, and charge him accordingly. That's what he has been doing to me for years."

136. A long-winded bore was putting his friends to sleep with endless reminiscences about a trip to Switzerland. At last he concluded: "Gentlemen, there I stood, high up on a mountain with a great abyss yawning before me."

To which one irritated listener queried, "Was that abyss yawning before you got there?"

137. "A procrastinator," said an energetic businessman, "is a person who has hardening of the oughteries."

138. A weather forecaster in Little Rock, Arkansas, reported that there had been a violent dust storm in the southern Midwest. He cautioned, "Many surfaces such as cars and patio furniture may be coated with a thin layer of Texas and Oklahoma."

139. The football coach of a small school, which hadn't had a good season for several years, pondered what to say to his team at a pep rally. Finally, he spoke: "All right, men, here we are, unbeaten, untied, and unscored upon. Let's get out there! We're ready for our first game!"

140. A poor man, out of a job, was walking through a cemetery when he came to a large, ornate, grandiose tomb. He gazed at it with great admiration, slowly shook his head, and muttered, "Now *that's* what I call living!"

141. At high-quality colleges, where the professors tend to consider themselves sources of truth who owe reverence to no one—not even the president—well-phrased insults to authority are occasionally heard. A good example is the remark of Professor Arnold Post to President Felix Morely of Haverford College, after Morely had made a report to the faculty: "Sir, verbosity may be your long suit, but it's not long enough to cover your asininity."

142. In the Old South, a gentleman visited the hut of a poor farmer. He entered just as a roaring thunderstorm began and rain poured through the roof. "Hey," shouted the gent, "it's leaking in here!"

"No, Sir," replied the farmer. "It's leaking outside. It's *raining* in here."

143. Some brief ads are wittily effective, especially in their honesty. Here's one someone sent me from the Chico, California, *Enterprise-Record:*

FREE TO A GOOD HOME—Pip, male Pointer mix, six months old, neutered. Needs someone to play fetch, Frisbee, maybe go hunting. Present owners are too pooped for Pip.

5

Family Relations

The subject of family relations follows the topic of language quite naturally. In some families you have to "watch your language," but in a really loving family there is more language freedom than in the outside world. A small child may say, with a smile, "I farted," within the family, but that child should be made aware that you don't say that in somebody else's house, or in public.

Strained Relations

144. Warnings of an earthquake in California induced a couple to send their young son out of state to stay with an aunt and uncle. A few days later, the couple found a message on their telephone answering device: "We are returning your son. Please send the earthquake instead."

145. Little Abigail was sitting on a park bench crying and sobbing. A neighbor happened to come by and asked her, "What's the matter, Abigail?"

Through her tears she cried, "My mom has lost her book on child-raising."

"That's not too bad," said the neighbor. "There's no reason to be so upset, is there?"

"Oh, yes," sobbed Abigail. "Now Mom's using her own judgment."

146. A teenager named Don was asked how he'd enjoyed his recent fishing expedition with his dad. Don replied, "It was a disaster. I did absolutely everything wrong: I talked too loud; I used the wrong bait; I cast in bad places; I reeled in too soon; and—worst of all—I caught more than Dad did."

147. A precocious but ungainly little boy rushed into the kitchen and shouted, "Mom!"

"Yes, dear?" asked his mother.

"You know that beautiful vase in the living room that you're always telling me has been handed down from generation to generation?"

"Yes," replied his mother, holding her breath. "What about it?"

"Well, Mom," said the boy, "the last generation has dropped it."

148. Joe Speller went off on a month's vacation with his family. When he returned to the office, a fellow worker asked, "Well, how did you enjoy your trip?"

"Hmm, wh—," mumbled Joe.

"What's the matter?" asked his friend. "Didn't you have a good time?"

"Well," said Joe, "have you ever spent four weeks in a station wagon with those you thought you loved best?"

149. Some good friends of mine still enjoy talking, especially at the dinner table. But if a family member goes on too long, it's understood that he or she will stop if someone says distinctly, "NOGI." What's it mean? "Not of General Interest."

Now that the kids are off to college, the parents have a new dog, and everyone agreed to name him Nogi.

150. A mother of several young, vigorous children had had a trying day and was feeling annoyed and angry. She was a religious person, however, and so, as she felt herself nearing the breaking point, she looked upward, clasped her hands, and prayed, "Dear Lord, grant me patience—but for God's sake hurry!"

FAMILY RELATIONS 67

151. This is a true story about the ten-year-old daughter of two college professors. One day, Juliet was acting in a very objectionable way, and her mother, never at a loss for big words, said, "Okay, Julie, stop it! I'm getting fed up with your juvenility."

"Yeah?" retorted Julie. "Well, I want you to know I often get fed up with your adultery."

152. A teenager was trying on a dress. She admired herself in the mirror and then said to the saleslady, "This dress is wonderful! I love it! I'll buy it."

"Fine," said the saleslady, and then noticed that the girl was hesitating. After a moment she asked, "Well, uh, in case Mom likes it, can I bring it back?"

153. Perhaps it's understandable why some children don't always believe their parents. A mother shouted at her son, "I've told you a million times not to exaggerate!"

154. Mr. Bowes came home from work and found his son sitting on the front steps looking angry and unhappy.

"What's wrong, Jimmy? You look terrible," said Mr. Bowes.

His son replied, "Wrong? Nothing—I just can't get along with your wife!"

155. It is reliably reported that William James (1842-1910) employed his daughter to prepare the index for one of his books. It may have been *Principles of Psychology* (1890), or *The Will to Believe* (1897), or *The Varieties of Religious Experience* (1902)—I don't know. However, while working in one of the books, the daughter grew somewhat bitter because she was not paid. So she sneaked in this index entry: birds, for the, 3-499.

I suppose the proofreader caught the mischief before publication.

Pure Love

Some family relationships are based on what seems like pure love, which is not to say that bursts of anger are not a part of caring and love. What could be duller than "We've been married for thirty years and have never had a cross word"? But here are three "pure love" stories, one involving a non-human.

> **156.** A young mother was walking home from the local grocery store carrying shopping bags and accompanied by her four small, lively, vociferous children. An older man met her, smiled admiringly, and asked, "How do you ever manage to divide your love among those four wriggly, cute, demanding kids?"
>
> Answered the mother, "I don't divide it. I multiply it."

> **157.** A proud mother was wheeling her six-month-old baby down the street when two women passers-by remarked, "What a beautiful baby! How cute and responsive!"
>
> The mother smiled and replied, "If you like the baby, wait till you see the pictures!"

(Note: If you're ever in a situation where you feel compelled to comment on a not-very-attractive baby to its mother, a foolproof response is: "My, that *is* a baby!")

> **158.** A third-grader was given an assignment to write on the subject "What My Dog Means to Me." He wrote:

My dog means somebody nice and quiet to be with. He does not say "Do" like my mother, or "Don't" like my father, or "Stop" like my big brother. My dog Spot and I sit together quietly and I like him and he likes me.

Some Blunt Assessments

> **159.** After enjoying a long afternoon together, a father and his little daughter came home around suppertime.

"Well," said the mother, "you're late. Did you have fun with Dad?"

"Oh, yes, Mommy," said the girl. "And at the end we stopped in this place where I had a coke and Daddy had a glass of water with an olive in it."

160. Here's a new version of the classic explanation of baldness (that grass doesn't grow on a busy street):

Ozzie asked, "Mom, why doesn't Dad have hair on his head?"

"It's because he thinks a great deal, Dear," explained his mother.

"But, Mom," Ozzie pressed on, "how come you have so much hair on your head?"

(Note: An opposite version of the "busy street" explanation is: Why bother to put a new roof on an empty shed?)

161. Mrs. Potts's son had recently married in Philadelphia and moved with his wife to Seattle. A friend asked, "Have you traveled out to visit them yet?"

"No," said Mrs. Potts, "not yet."

"How come?" asked the friend. "Too expensive?"

"No," said Mrs. Potts again. "I'm waiting for them to have their first baby."

"Oh?" said the friend.

"Yes," said Mrs. Potts. "You see, I have a theory that grandmas are more welcome than mothers-in-law."

162. P. G. Wodehouse (1881-1975), whose comic novels concerned the aristocratic Bertie Wooster and his unflappable valet Jeeves, dedicated one of his books thus: "To my wife and daughter without whose unfailing help and advice this book could have been written in half the time."

163. I am a firm believer in evolution. The earth and all its creatures were not made in six days with Sunday off. However, sometimes I have to question the wisdom of evolution's designs, especially when I observe my female children, and *their* children. I am impressed—

even amazed—at what challenges mothers must meet, what with the kids, the housework, and even a job. It makes me think that evolution would have been more effective if mothers had more than two hands.

164. When Manny Tyndale came home from work, he found his wife Lydia in tears.

"Darling," he asked, "What is the matter?"

"I've been insulted," she sobbed, "insulted by your mother."

"But how could that be? She's way out in Kansas, and she never telephones," said Manny.

"Yes, yes, I know," said Lydia, "but a letter came for you this morning, and I opened it."

"Oh, I see," said Manny. "But how did she insult you?"

"She wrote a P.S.," replied Lydia. "It said, 'Dear Lydia, don't forget to give this letter to Manny.'"

165. The young boy ran into the house. "Mommy, Dad fell off the ladder!"

"Oh, goodness!" said the mother. "Is he all right?"

"Yeah. Don't worry, Mom," said the boy. "He's just talking to himself."

"What's he saying?"

"Shall I leave out the naughty words?" asked the boy.

"Of course," said Mom.

"Nothing," smiled the boy.

166. Someone made this observation about a modern, health-oriented family with two working parents: "The children run through the house eating yogurt, sunflower seeds, cereal, partly because this is healthy, and partly because no one has time to cook."

167. The teacher asked a little girl who was in school for the first time, "What is your name?"

"Laura Don't," replied the girl.

Apparently, that's all she ever heard at home. Bad girl or bad parents?

Ingenious Tricks for Busy Family Members

168. A gifted young student came home from school one day and found a note in the hall: "Greg: I had to go out. Please help me by wiping up the H_2O that got spilled on the kitchen floor.—Mom."

Greg didn't feel like doing domestic chores, and when he saw the spill in the kitchen, he was even less willing; so he wrote below the note: "Mom, this is not H_2O. It's K_9P.—Greg," and he went out to play.

169. Hard-working househusband to a friend: "Boy, I sure do find these Do-It-Yourself books useful."

Friend: "Me, too, but I've thought up a subject for a book that will make me millions when I get it written."

Househusband: "What'll it be called?"

Friend: *"How to Get Out of Doing It Yourself."*

170. An Irish immigrant woman had worked as the cook for an elegant upper-class family for many years. One day the family dog died, and everyone, including the cook, was very sad. A member of the family overheard her in the kitchen commiserating with the butler: "Sure, and isn't meself that's sorry the dog died. 'Tis many a dish he saved me the washing of."

6

Married Life and Children

It occurs to me that this chapter on married life and children should have come before the one on family relations. After all, one hopes that most couples will get married before they have kids. But then, two chapters from now I deal with the humorous aspects of sex and reproduction—so conclude what you wish from that.

By the Authority Invested in . . .

171. Justice Felix Frankfurter (1882–1965) was asked by a good friend to officiate at the friend's wedding ceremony.

"I'm sorry," said Frankfurter. "I'd really like to, but I do not have the authority to marry people."

"I can't believe it!" exclaimed the friend. "A Justice of the Supreme Court doesn't have that authority? How come?"

"Well," said Frankfurter, "I suppose it's because marriage is not considered a federal offense."

Lovers' Quarrels

Of course married life doesn't have to be a federal offense to have a variety of problems, to wit:

172. In marriage, it's quite normal to argue now and then, even to shout. One happily married couple were having a strong argument as they sat in front of the fireplace. During a lull in the action, the wife looked at their cat and dog sleepily and quietly enjoying the warmth of the fire. The wife resumed, "Look at them. Why can't we get along happily and peacefully like that?"

"Hmm?" said the husband. "Well, just tie them together and see what happens."

173. Mr. and Mrs. Loomis had a terrible argument in the car while on a long trip together. The shouting finally stopped, and they both sat fuming in silence while staring distractedly at the rural scenery passing by. Pointing to a mule in a field, Mr. Loomis asked his wife with sarcastic emphasis: "Oh, *darling*? Isn't that a relative of yours?"

"Why, yes, *dear*," she snapped back. "By marriage."

174. The Garretts were having a fierce quarrel, and Mr. Garrett was on the verge of losing his temper. He warned his wife, "You'd better be careful, or you'll bring out the beast in me!"

Unimpressed, Mrs. Garret retorted, "So what? Who's afraid of mice?"

175. Exasperated by her dillydallying, Mark called upstairs to his wife, "For the last time, Pamela, are you coming?"

To which Pamela replied, "Yes, dear. Haven't I been telling you for the last hour I'll be down in a minute?"

The Modern Approach

176. Even such solemn and joyous traditional occasions as weddings are getting pretty modern these days. For example, after marrying the bride and groom with the traditional words—"I now pronounce you husband

and wife"—the minister added, "And if you have any problems, call my 800 number."

177. These days, many people's views of marriage are different from those prevalent a generation or two ago. For example, a bride was preparing for the big event with her bridesmaids, when one of them nonchalantly asked her, "Are you planning a long marriage after the ceremony?"

Two Sage Opinions

178. The great Greek philosopher and teacher Socrates (469-399 B.C.) was once asked by a disciple, "Is it good for a man to marry?"
Socrates replied, "Yes, it is good. If he has the good fortune to find a woman who is beautiful and loving, his life will be greatly enriched. But if, on the contrary, he should marry a shrew, like my own Xantippe, then he will become a philosopher."

179. Lewis Mumford (1895-1990), a great American social philosopher, educator, and observer of the cultures of cities and civilizations, was also a great classifier and organizer. In addition, he was not a "faithful" husband. He wrote that he was "romantically in love" with one woman; "intellectually in love" with another; and "domestically in love" with his wife Sophia.

Children and Their Antics

180. A grandfather who had eight female grandchildren eagerly awaited grandchild number nine. When the baby was born, he called the father to find out what gender the child was.
"What's the news?" asked Grandma, his wife.
"Alas, a lass," he replied.

Alas, a lass? Alas, children? Well, of course not. And what could be more delightful than the behavior of children and what children themselves say about it?

181. Willie's mother introduced him to a visitor.

The visitor asked, "How old are you, young man?"

"I'm at an awkward age," he replied.

"Oh?" said the visitor. "Why awkward?"

"Well," Willie said, "I'm too old to cry and too young to swear."

182. An ambitious, well-brought-up young girl was earnestly writing on a piece of paper. Her two-and-a-half-year-old brother asked, "Watcha doing, Anna?"

"I'm making a five-year plan for reaching the important goals in my life," replied Anna. "See, kiddo. One, two, three, four, and five."

"Oh," said her little brother. "Well, me, I just live one diaper at a time."

183. Some youngsters are fairly—but not totally—conscientious about praying. One small girl was heard to say, "Dear Lord, if you can't make me a gooder girl, don't worry too much about it. I'm having a real good time like I am!"

And a young boy suddenly whistled in church. As soon as the service was over, his mother scolded him, and asked, "Whatever made you do such a thing?"

"Well, Mom," he replied, "I prayed to God to show me how to whistle, and right there in church He did."

184. A small boy named Kenny came home from school looking terrible. His father asked, "Kenny, what happened?"

"I got beaten up by Barbara," sniffed Kenny.

"What!" said his father, "you let yourself get beaten up by a mere girl?"

"Well, Dad," explained Kenny, "girls aren't nearly as mere as they used to be."

185. During fifth-grade recess, the playground tough egg pointed out a cute pig-tailed classmate to one of his cronies and said, "If I ever stop hating girls, she's the one I'm going to stop hating first."

Shenanigans

186. A small boy was making a nuisance of himself during an airplane flight. He was yelling, running up and down the aisle, and bumping into people, while his parents paid no attention. When the flight attendant served coffee, he ran into the serving cart and knocked several cups of coffee to the floor.

With murder in her eyes, the flight attendant glared at the parents and said, "May I make a suggestion?"

"Oh, certainly," said the parents with smiling, vapid faces.

"Send that kid outside to play!"

187. Peter Ustinov (1921-   ) is a philosopher, actor, and writer. His works include *Dear Me, My Russia,* and *The Wit of Peter Ustinov.* He said, "My children often disagreed with me, thank God! I'd no objection at all to their being disobedient. Parents should remember that besides being parents, they are also the bone on which the puppy can shape its teeth.

So, parents, don't permit total confusion, but remember that you are—in a sense you often may not recognize—the instruments of your children's strength for the future.

Wives on Husbands, Husbands on Wives

188. During coffee break at the office two young women were talking together about life in general and their own future plans. One said to the other, "Yes, when I get married, I want to have children, but I don't want my husband to be one of them."

189. Mr. Shallcross's wife was sick in bed, and he had to do all the cooking. There was nearly total confusion. He couldn't even find the tea. In desperation, he called to his wife upstairs, "Where's the tea, dear? I just can't find it."

"I don't know why you can't find it," Mrs. Shallcross replied in annoyance. "It's in the top left cupboard in a cocoa can marked 'matches.'"

190. If you don't want to become a "has been," remember that variety is the spice of life. This is illustrated by the reaction of Mrs. Gratwick to her husband's behavior. She said, "George Gratwick, I can't figure you out. Monday you liked beans, Tuesday you liked beans, and Wednesday you liked beans, but now, all of a sudden, on Thursday, you *don't* like beans."

191. Mr. McCully was happily married—no doubt of that—but occasionally he seemed a bit tired and discouraged. A friend asked, "What's the matter, McCully? You don't seem quite as vigorous as you were before you got married."

"Well," said McCully, "I love my wife, but occasionally—well, I find that she has a whim of iron."

192. Two women were discussing their spouses' work:
"Just what does your husband do?"
"He's an expediter."
"What's that?"
"Well, if we women did what he does, it'd be called nagging."

193. Two suburban ladies who were neighbors were having mid-morning coffee.

"Myra," said Nancy, "you always seem to have such wonderful clothes, and I can't get my husband to kick in with any money at all for such things. Do you have some kind of special technique?"

"In a way, I have. I had the same problem as you. One morning while he was still in bed I walked into the room stark naked with my shopping bag in my hand.

I told him I was going to the supermarket. He said, 'Like that?' I said, 'Like this.' I added that since he refused to give me money for decent clothes, this was the way I was going to do my shopping from now on. He kissed me and gave me a hundred dollars. "Why don't you try it on Walt, Nancy?"

Nancy did. One morning she entered the bedroom naked, with shopping bag in hand. He looked at her and said, "Where the hell do you think you're going?"

"Shopping, at the supermarket," replied Nancy.

"Well," he growled, "you might at least shave."

194. One of the most useful ways married couples can help each other is in finding things their partners have lost. The best question is When did you last use it—in the car? in the cellar? out in the yard?, etc. One has to be careful, though, lest a bit of sarcasm creep in. Example: A husband was working on a very difficult home-improvement project which entailed much snarling and swearing. At one point, he exclaimed, "I think I've lost my mind!"

His wife responded sweetly, "When did you last use it?"

195. After a large social gathering, Mr. Longstretch said to his wife, "It seems to me that there are two kinds of people at every party."

"What do you mean, Dear?" asked his wife.

"Well," he replied, "There are those who want to leave early and those who don't. And the trouble is, they're married to each other."

Kids Will Be Kids

196. A young girl kept a diary of her family trip across the USA. Each night she wrote a few words about the day's happenings. She was really impressed by the Grand Canyon, especially the north rim, and after supper wrote quickly in the diary. When she'd gone to sleep, her father looked at what his daughter had written. It was: "Today I spit more than a mile."

197. Two couples and their children went on a picnic together. The little girl from the one family needed to pee, so her mother sent her behind some nearby bushes. Almost at once, the little boy from the other family had the same need and was dispatched to the same place. A few moments later the little girl was heard to say quite cheerfully, "Oh, that's a handy little gadget to bring along on a picnic!"

7

Smart Kid Answers—I

One of the delights of life is witty kids, even sassy (not nasty) kids. As I was putting this book together, I realized that there were quite a large number of "smart kid answers" among the stories I've been collecting over the years. There seemed to be enough for three short, book-punctuating chapters. This is the first, and it comes between Married Life and Sex, but don't expect any neat transition.

198. Young Ronald was being scolded by his mother and father for his low grades. His classmate Stevie, who lived next door, was held up as an example. "Stevie doesn't get C's and D's, does he?" said Ronald's father.

"No, Dad," replied Ronald, "but he's different. He has very bright parents."

199. Six-year-old Arthur didn't seem to hesitate to tell lies, even though his parents scolded and punished him when he did. One day, when he'd told an outrageous lie, his father said, "Art, I never told lies when I was your age."

Arthur thought for a moment and then, full of inquisitiveness, asked, "How old were you when you started, Dad?"

200. A fourth-grade class was studying inventions in a unit on science. The teacher, hoping to challenge the class, asked, "Can anyone tell us something really important that did not exist twenty-five years ago?"

A pupil raised his hand quickly.
"Yes, Mike?"
"Me!" replied Mike.

201. A sixth-grade class had had a picture taken of the whole group, and Mr. Ornston, the teacher, was persuading them to buy copies. He said, "Just think, years from now you'll be able to say, 'That's Nelson; he runs a business in Alabama'; 'That's Ellie; she's got four children and is also a lawyer.'"

Mr. Ornston paused, and a voice right up in front said, "And 'There's Mr. Ornston; he's dead.'"

202. A kindergartner came home from school one day looking both happy and a bit worried. Her mother asked her what had happened, and she replied, "The whole class broke out in jokes."

203. A five-year-old girl was asked by an older friend, "What do you do to earn your allowance?"

She replied earnestly, "I keep my mother occupied."

204. Matthew was a smart kid, and he didn't much like going to Sunday School. One day the teacher directed a question to him. "Matthew, who was Moses's mother?"

"Pharaoh's daughter," replied the boy.

"Now, Matt, you know that isn't right. Pharaoh's daughter found him in the bullrushes," the teacher stated.

"Yeah," said Matthew. "That's what *she* said!"

205. The Sunday School teacher had finished her talk on how people behave and what they must do to go to heaven. There was time for discussion, and she asked, "All right, who can tell us what we must do before we can be forgiven our sins?"

Gerald raised his hand and then said, "We've gotta sin."

206. A family was leaving the church after Sunday services and, as usual, greeting the minister at the door. A small boy shook the preacher's hand and asked, in a rather loud voice, "How come you know so much about sin?"

207. A very verbal three-year-old Ariana, who was brought up in a home where her parents taught quite naturally all the correct names for the parts of the body, saw a TV program which showed a cougar giving birth.

"Mom, look!" said Ariana, "the baby cougar came out of the mama cougar's anus!"

"No, Dear," said Ariana's mother, "not her anus, her vagina."

"Oh," said Ariana, "what a wonderful idea!"

(Note: This is a true story, told to me by leading sex educator Doctor Mary Steichen Calderone. Ariana is her granddaughter.)

And so with sin and the birth of cougars, we move smoothly into the next chapter.

8

Sex

Dangerous Liaisons

208. Fireflies have a spectacular, complex system of enabling males and females to find each other at night. They do it by means of flashes separated by periods of darkness. Each species has its own code, so that a firefly never says "Come hither" to the wrong species.

However, there is one species, the Photuris, the females of which can emit a copy of another species. When the male of that species, called the Photinus, is fooled and lands beside the Photuris female, instead of the anticipated sexual encounter, he is pounced upon and eaten.

Praying mantis females can be equally dangerous to males. In order to ensure a really vigorous ejaculation and genuine fertilization, at the climax of intercourse the female bites the head off her mate. She might be called a "voracious predator"!

All of which brings to mind a poem by Ogden Nash (1902-1971) called *The Firefly*:

> The firefly's flame
> Is something for which science has no name.
> I can think of nothing eerier
> Than flying around with an unidentified glow on a
>   person's posteerier.

Bestiality

209. An elderly Quaker friend of mine, knowing that I was involved in sex education and being very broad-minded, sent me what she called a "fucking joke."

A mouse, a regular at a certain bar, crawled up on a barstool and asked for a drink. Then he looked down to the end of the bar and saw a most elegant female giraffe leaning against the wall. When his drink was brought to him, the mouse asked the bartender to take a drink to this gorgeous creature and tell her that he had ordered it for her. When she received it, she looked at him and he looked at her, and he went down and joined her. They hit it off right away, and after lively conversation, left the bar together.

Late the next morning, the mouse appeared at the bar again. The bartender remarked to the mouse, "You look completely worn out and bedraggled. What happened?"

"Well," said the mouse, "between kissing and fucking, I must have run a hundred miles!"

Turn-ons and Turn-offs

210. Two Nantucket spinsters lived together for many years. They had lots of female cats, but carefully brought them all in at night to keep them out of trouble. But at last, one of the spinsters got married and left the house. A few days later the remaining spinster received a postcard from her friend. It read, "Let the cats out."

211. Hortense was telling Mabel about a date she had had the night before with a handsome, eligible bachelor. Mabel asked, "Did he give you the famous come-hither look?"

"No," replied Hortense, "it was more like stay thither."

212. A young farmer was walking in the pasture with his lady love. They came upon his prize bull serving a heifer which was in season. Noticing his girl was watching with considerable interest, he screwed up his courage and said, "I think it would be fun to do that."

"Well, it's your cow," she replied.

213. A young woman was preparing for a date. She went to a cosmetics shop and asked, "Do you have any green lipstick?"

The clerk looked puzzled. "Green lipstick?" he asked.

"Yes, green," the woman said. "Tonight I'm going out with a railroad man."

214. An eccentric, single-minded woman purchased some panties. She asked the salesperson, "Could I have a sentence embroidered on them?"

"Certainly, I think we can manage that," said the salesperson. "What do you want the sentence to say?"

" 'If you can read this, you're too damned close,' " the woman said.

"Do you want block or script letters?" asked the salesperson.

"Braille," said the woman.

Doing and Not Doing It: Two Limericks

215. This limerick raises some fascinating sexual questions and also is a triumph of correct grammatical construction.

> There was a gay man named Bloom
> Who took a lesbian up to his room.
>   They argued all night
>   As to who had the right
> To do what, with which, and to whom.

216. These days, despite modern techniques, we seem to have a good many females who get pregnant at a very young age. The following old limerick suggests how to avoid it.

There was a young lady named Wild,
Who managed to stay undefiled
　　By thinking of Jesus,
　　Contagious diseases,
And the danger of having a child.

From the Annals of Sex Disorders: Runny Noses and Smoking Body Parts

217. Today, we hear a good deal about problems of sex. Did you know, for example, that sexual intercourse can bring on attacks of vasomotor rhinitis. Yes, it can cause inflammation of the nasal mucosa associated with the parasympathetic nervous system. This problem can be difficult to treat, according to Dr. Jeffrey Wald of San Diego, California.

In short, sex can stimulate sneezing. (But don't sneeze at sex!)

218. A sex counselor was trying to get a few facts straight about a female patient so that he could help her. He asked, "Mrs. Maxwell, do you smoke after you have sexual intercourse?"

"I don't know," replied Mrs. Maxwell, "I've never looked."

Only Skin Deep

219. A man who was very fastidious about keeping his body in perfect shape by jogging, weight-lifting, and sunbathing, looked in the mirror one morning and saw that he was well-tanned everywhere except his penis. So, being an extremist, he went to a nude beach and buried his whole body in the sand, except for his penis. As he lay there, he heard the voices of two old ladies approaching. One said: "There is really no justice in this world."

"What do you mean, my dear?" asked the other.

"Well, just look at that!" exclaimed the first lady,

pointing at the man's penis. "When I was ten years old, I was afraid of it. When I was 20, I was curious about it. When I was 30, I enjoyed it. When I was 40, I asked for it. When I was 60, I prayed for it. When I was 70, I forgot about it. Now that I'm 80, the damn things are growing wild along the beach."

220. I suppose most women would like to be beautiful, just as most men would like to be extremely handsome. Well, think again about the lives of gorgeous women. Here are comments by three of them:

Actress Jaclyn Smith says beauty causes too many men to want to be friends. She is approached in stores, on the street, and is even followed home. When she doesn't respond, she is chided for being rude.

Former Miss America Phyllis George reports that a beauty has to try ten times harder because so many people assume that if you are beautiful you must also be dumb.

Actress Cybill Shepherd said: "Beauty isn't the solution some people think. It's actually a whole new set of problems. The way I look makes communication with women as well as men difficult. Often people are so involved with my appearance, they don't listen to what I say, so I end up watching them watch me talk."

Maybe cosmetics departments should start selling uglification products. A new market?

Flings, Affairs, and Quickies

221. A business tycoon was sitting at a bar when a young woman came in and sat next to him. After a bit of conversation, he offered her $1000 to spend the weekend with him at his home. She accepted. After the weekend she asked for the money, and he said he would mail her a check.

When the check arrived, it was only for $500, so she called on him at his office. Not wanting to embarrass him in front of other people, she said, "In regard to that house you rented—I only received half the rent."

The man, catching on, said, "Oh yes, the house, well, in the first place, you didn't tell me it had been used. In the second place, it was too big, and in the third place, there was no heat."

She quickly retorted: "In the first place, you didn't ask if it had been used. In the second place, it wasn't too big, you just didn't have enough furniture to fill it. And in the third place, there was plenty of heat—you just didn't know how to turn it on."

She got the second $500.

222. Different women have different views about sexual intercourse. Here are three:

Prostitute: "When's this gonna be over?"

Girlfriend: "I hope this never ends."

Wife: "I think I'll paint the ceiling white."

223. A man confided in a friend, "Gee, I'm scared! I got a letter from a fellow who says if I don't stay away from his wife, he'll shoot me."

"Well," said his friend, "all you've got to do is stay away."

"Yeah," said the man, "but he didn't sign his name."

224. A man from Philadelphia asked a taxi driver in Boston, "Do you know where I can get scrod*?"

"Sure," replied the driver, "but it's the first time I ever heard it in the past pluperfect."

Learning about Sex

225. Two teenagers, aged 15, tried to get married at city hall but were refused a marriage license. So the boy asked, "Well, then, can we have a learner's permit?"

---

*Young cod or halibut, much served in the Boston area.

226. Mrs. Sinkler was handing out the first report cards of the year to her sixth-grade class. After seeing her grades, Jenny waved her hand vigorously with a scowl on her face.

"What's wrong, Jenny?" asked Mrs. Sinkler. "Aren't you satisfied with your grades?"

"No, I'm not!" exclaimed Jenny. "You gave me an F in sex and I didn't even know I was taking it."

Some Memorable Quips

227. George Bernard Shaw (1856–1950), the prolific Irish playwright and critic, was famed for his wit and irreverence. He said, "Why should we take advice on sex from the Pope? If he knows anything about it, he shouldn't."

228. When someone asked Winston Churchill (1874–1965) what the main difference between a man and a woman is, he paused a moment and then said, "I can't conceive."

229. An uncle of mine, Carroll Taylor, a well-known and successful lawyer, a vigorous, humorous character, and a very happily married man, did have some views about females. One of them was: "The world is flat and covered with nervous women." Another view also included how to get out of the Great Depression. Uncle Carroll said, "It's simple. Just put all the women in the world on one continent and all the men on another, and everybody will be busy building boats." (We nephews used to call it the BBB theory.)

Double Entendre

230. I have written a number of sex-education books for children and adults. In the course of conducting research for these works, I bought a book titled *Medical Aspects of Human Sexuality*, published by Clinical

Communications, Inc., of New York. A notice in small print on the coyright page struck me as accidentally amusing: "Reproduction without specific permission is prohibited."

The Population Bomb

Now consider two comments on a serious result of sexuality.

231. Pacific salmon are famed for their grueling journeys of hundreds of miles to reach their headwater breeding grounds. A father was explaining this to his boy, a youngster who had been taught to be deeply concerned about the world's overpopulation problem. The father said, "Salmon swim hundreds of miles upstream, against strong currents, and even past fishermen trying to spear them. And then they have to leap up waterfalls. Only then can they spawn and have children."

"Wow!" said the boy. "That might be a good idea for human beings!"

232. Two friends were discussing the world's problem of overpopulation. One said, "The population explosion is a problem with no solution."

"But why?" asked his friend.

"Because," he replied, "it's so much fun lighting the fuse."

Four-Letter Words

233. A good close for this chapter will be an essay written by Steven Briggs, who in 1977 was in a sex-education class of mine at Germantown Friends School in Philadelphia. The assignment was to write on sex and language, and before it was made we had discussed a good many "four-letter-words."

EXPRESSING SEX IN FOUR-LETTER WORDS

Sex is a word that we usually do not use in public or around the family. Some people feel embarrassed when they or someone else talks about sex. So they use other words to tell what they mean. They use words such as *help*. This word means that a man and a woman have to help themselves to remember to use contraceptives and to help themselves to achieve their orgasm.

The four-letter word *give* would mean that they would have to give each other their support.

Care, another 4-letter word, would mean for them to care for themselves and for their children.

And *kiss*—that would mean that they would promise to kiss each other in the morning before they go out and at night before they go to bed.

Feel—this would mean that they would have to care for each other's feelings, and to feel each other to show that they love each other and to get confidence with his or her partner.

Love—still 4 letters—would mean that they would love each other always and be faithful to each other and show their love during intercourse and in the home.

9

Problems of Life

234. Life would be dull if it gave us no problems, yes? But one of the best ways to live with problems, or to solve them, is to see their humorous side. The kind of humor described by William Morris Davis (1850–1934), American geographer, geologist, and founder of the Association of American Geographers, is helpful for problem solving: "The kind of humor I like is the thing that makes me laugh for five seconds and think for ten minutes."

Think about it!

Don't Take Problems Too Seriously

235. Here are some concise views about love, life, and marriage stated by four women who should know (in chronological order):

- Agatha Christie (1891–1976), author of over 80 books: "An archeologist is the best husband any woman can have. The older she gets, the more he is interested in her!"

- Mae West (1892–1980): "Between two evils, I always pick the one I never tried before."

- Tallulah Bankhead (1903–1968): "If I had my life to live again, I'd make the same mistakes, only sooner."

- Cherilyn Sarkisian (1946-   ), otherwise known as Cher: "The trouble with some women is that they get all excited about nothing—and then marry him."

236. Norman Vincent Peale (1898-   ) met a friend in New York who went on and on about how terrible his life was, nothing but misery and problems. Finally Peale said, "Friend, I know a place in the Bronx where there are 25,000 people with no problems."

"Oh, Norman, take me there!" said his friend.

"You're sure you want to go?" said Peale. "It's the Woodlawn Cemetery."

The Naive Approach to Problem Solving

237. Naiveté can be a way to attack problems, but it usually doesn't work. The service department of a telephone company received a call from an elderly woman.

"I have a request to make, please," she said.

"Yes?" replied the service representative.

"My telephone cord is too long and I'm always tripping over it. Would you please pull it back at your end?"

238. Two earnest-looking teenage girls were talking seriously in the living room about life and its problems. "You know what I think?" said Margarita.

"What?" asked Helen.

"I think the age of twenty-five should be lowered to eighteen."

239. Four-year-old Nick asked his father, "When I grow up, will I have to go to work?"

His father replied, "I'm afraid so, son."

Nick continued: "What will I do when I get there, Dad?"

The Healing Profession

Doctors are supposed to help us with our problems. Two of my children are doctors, so I respect the medical profession and I like my own doctor, too.

> **240.** A doctor was reviewing the facts of his patient's case. He said, "Hmm, let me see: mild depression, low energy, fatigue, sore knees, easy irritation, weight gain. It sounds to me that you have a serious case of adulthood."

> **241.** There were two psychiatrists, one fairly old, the other quite young. At the end of each day, the young doctor appeared worried and weary, even distressed, while the older man seemed fresh and alive.
> "How do you do it?" asked the young doctor. "'You always look great at the end of the day."
> The older psychiatrist replied, "I never listen."

> **242.** Some cynic was asked what the job of the psychiatrist is. He replied, "It's the search for the id by the odd."

Dealing with Phobias

> **243.** Phobias are terrible things, if severe. But they have their lighter side. For example, I've typed much of this book on an old hand-powered Hermes portable, or given my scribbles to a marvelous typist to transcribe. Why not use a word processor? Because I'm a *cyberphobic* (one who's afraid of electronic devices).
> But do you know about people with *triskaidekaphobia*? It comes from the Greek words meaning "three-and-10 fear." These folks were glad to know that 1988 had only one Friday the 13th, whereas 1989, 1990, and 1991 had two. Use it to have some fun with the number 13.
> If you're a teacher, ask your students to find a word with 13 letters; to share something new and interesting in volume 13 of an encyclopedia; to read about the 13th president or the 13th state; to estimate the weight of

13 students; to find a constellation with 13 stars; or to list items on the back of a dollar bill that are grouped in sets of 13 (the shield on the eagle's breast has 13 stripes; the eagle's right claw holds an olive branch with 13 leaves, and the left claw holds 13 arrows; the motto "e pluribus unum" has 13 letters).

Vive 13!

244. I remember that my mother hated the clutter that seemed to occupy every nook and cranny of our family's house. She had a theory that any horizontal space in a house will inevitably become occupied with stuff; she said her ideal house would be one full of closets, all of them empty.

Recently, I saw an item that made me realize that this was not just an idiosyncrasy of the Johnson family but a more general human problem. The item was in a list of evening courses given by the Community College of Pennsylvania. In their fall 1990 catalog, titled *Expand Your World,* was a course: "Managing Clutter," given by Wallace Wilkins, Ph.D., a psychologist whose practice focuses on "reducing self-defeating habits and moods." Here's the description of the course:

Are you overwhelmed by the continuing build-up of clutter in your home? Do you feel tense and anxious about your inability to handle this problem?

If you have difficulty getting rid of newspaper articles, old clothes, books, or material objects, then a workshop on managing clutter may be the answer . . . .

Topics include:

• Reasons for accumulating clutter

• Separating from the past

• Organizing your papers, files, closets

• A step-by-step action plan and more!

The Big Picture

Keeping the world and yourself—or even the universe—in perspective helps deal with problems.

> **245.** When I walk across my little part of the world, I often think—because I'm not thinking—that I am at the center of the universe and at times am even tempted to join the Flat Earth Society. But I've traveled around the world twice, so I guess it isn't flat.
>
> But it takes intelligence—even a sense of humor—to realize that the sun, if it were hollow, could contain over a million earths; that there are stars so large they could contain 500 million of "our" suns; that there are, maybe, 100 billion stars in the average galaxy *and* over 100 million galaxies in known (unknown?) space.
>
> It is good to think on these things in order to keep our sense of perspective. But I still can't help feeling that the center of the universe is at the ball point of my pen as I finish this story.

Note: If you feel too heavily weighed down by all this, consider that in the so-called "black holes" of space there are remnants of exploded stars which, some astronomers say, are so dense that a teaspoonful of their material may weigh a billion tons!

Playing with Money, Numbers, and the Truth

> **246.** After many celebrated escapades, a well-known roué finally squandered all of his money.
>
> "What happened?" asked a friend.
>
> "Well," said the ex-roué, "part of it went for liquor, part for fast cars, and a lot for women. The rest I spent foolishly."

> **247.** In the early fifties, a witty fellow who was good at statistics, arithmetic, and possibly distortion, reported these figures about the U.S.A.:

- total population: 163,000,000
- people over 65: 43,000,000
  - remainder: 120,000,000
- people under 21: 56,000,000
  - remainder: 64,000,000
- government employees: 27,000,000
  - remainder: 37,000,000
- armed forces: 12,000,000
  - remainder: 25,000,000
- city or state employees: 21,000,000
  - remainder: 4,000,000
- in hospitals or asylums: 3,800,000
  - remainder: 200,000
- street people: 175,000
  - remainder: 25,000
- in jail: 24,998
  - remainder to do the work: 2

You and me—and *I'm* getting tired!

248. Sometimes a person has to choose between weaknesses. This is especially true of fishermen, by their own account. There's a story about one fisherman who went into a fish shop and made a request to the man at the counter: "Please stand just where you are and throw me five good-sized trout."

"You want me to throw them?" asked the amazed counterman. "Why?"

"Because then I can tell my family I caught them," replied the fisherman. "I may be a lousy fisherman but I'm not a liar."

Put in His Place

249. A few years ago, Theodore Andrews wrote to a rural motel to ask if his dog would be allowed to stay there. He received this reply:

Dear Mr. Andrews:
  I have been in the motel business for over twenty years.

Never yet have I had to call in the police to eject a disorderly dog in the small hours of the morning. No dog has ever attempted to pass off a bad check on me. Never has a dog set the bedclothes afire through smoking. I have never found a hotel towel in a dog's suitcase. Your dog is welcome.

P.S.: If he will vouch for you, you can come too.

250. One of America's greatest football coaches was Vince Lombardi (1913-70), under whose command the Green Bay Packers (of Green Bay, Wisconsin) won five national championships in the 1960s. Well, even such famous people sometimes are put in their place, and this happened to Lombardi. He was at a restaurant, and a little boy approached his table. Lombardi reached for a menu and autographed it for the kid, but the youngster said, "I don't want a menu. I want to borrow the ketchup."

Big Trouble, Minor Complaints

251. Some years ago, a railroad engineer was having a difficult time getting his steam locomotive started. Finally he got his train going full-speed, sixty miles an hour, but the whistle wouldn't work; his hat blew out of the window; and steam leaked into the cabin. Then, as he was going around a sharp curve along a single track, he saw another train speeding toward him, only a few yards away. He turned to the coal shoveler and said, "George, did you ever have one of those days when everything seems to go wrong?"

252. Some years ago, three Soviet citizens were convicted of spying and sentenced to death. One was a Pole, one a Czech, and one a Jew. The judge granted each of them one last wish.

The Pole said, "I want my ashes scattered over the grave of Pilsudski."*

---

*Joseph Pilsudski(1867-1935), famous Polish general and politician.

The Czech said, "My ashes scatter over the grave of Masaryk.*

"Me," said the Jew, "I want my ashes scattered over the grave of Comrade Kosygin."†

"But that's impossible," he was told. "Kosygin isn't dead yet."

"I can wait," said the Jew.

253. A born skeptic, tired of hearing for the umpteenth time that George Washington (1732-1799) never told a lie, quipped, "It was easy then. He never filed a tax return or played golf."

254. A golfer, feeling very frustrated by his bad game, exclaimed, "I'd move heaven and earth to be able to break 100 on this course!"

"I suggest you try heaven," said his partner. "You've already moved most of the earth."

255. There are numerous ways to have trouble on the job but few are worse than what happened to a butcher. He backed into the meat slicer and got a little behind in his work.

Booklenders and Bookkeepers

I find that books and libraries solve lots of my difficult situations, and, since you are reading this book, probably you do too.

256. Libraries are my idea of paradise, and librarians, as a group, with their willingness to be helpful and their great caring about accuracy and detail, are the nearest things to saints that I know. For instance, if it had not been for the staff of the Free Library of Philadelphia, I might never have gotten some of the

---

*Thomas Garrigne Masaryk (1850-1947), principal founder and first president of Czechoslovakia.

†Alexsei Nikolayevich Kosygin (1904-1981), premier of the USSR council of ministers, 1964.

details of this book straight—and I did it all with them by telephone.

But this story concerns another library and its head, Dr. Vartan Gregorian (1934-   ). He once said, with joy: "Hell is a place where nothing is connected with anything else, but at the New York Public Library, we connect everything!"

257. Henry Wadsworth Longfellow (1807-1882) loved books and sometimes lent them to friends. His experiences caused him to comment, "I find that my friends are very poor arithmeticians but excellent bookkeepers." Perhaps if he had followed the practice of some monasteries in the ninth century he would have had better luck. Inside their precious books they put a curse, first stated by Juvenal (60?-140? A.D.), the Roman satiric poet. It read:

> Qui cupit hunc librum sibimet contendere privum, Hic flegetouteas patiatur sulphure flammas.

Translated by a later unknown versifier it reads:

> Whoe'r this book to make his own doth plot,
> The fires of hell and brimstone be his lot!

Feel free to use these at home or to recommend them to your local library!

258. Mark Twain (1835-1910) found a book in his neighbor's library. "May I borrow it?" he asked.

"You're welcome to read it any time, if you read it here," the neighbor said. "You see, I have a rule that books cannot leave these premises."

A few weeks later, the neighbor called on Twain and asked to borrow his lawn mower. "Certainly," said Twain, "but according to my rule, you must use it on these premises."

Does Honesty Pay?

259. A woman finally won a parrot at an auction after some very spirited bidding. As she took the bird, she said to the auctioneer, "I suppose the bird talks."

"Talks!?" said the auctioneer. "Who do you think has been bidding against you for the past half an hour?"

260. A man sat down at a table in a greasy-spoon restaurant. The waitress handed him a menu and said, "Sir, we have practically everything on the menu."

"So I see," said the man. "Can you bring me a clean one?"

261. A witness at a trial became very frustrated and turned to the judge. "Judge," he said, "I just don't know what to do."

"What do you mean?" asked the judge.

"Well, your honor," said the witness, "I swore to tell the truth, but every time I try, a lawyer objects."

Let Me Spell It Out for You

262. A little girl didn't want to go away to summer camp, but her parents were sure she'd like it and have some great experiences. To be sure she would keep in touch with her parents, her mother addressed and stamped several postcards and said, "All you have to do is write 'I'm fine' and mail one to Dad and me every few days."

The girl looked puzzled and thoughtful and then asked, "Mom?"

"Yes, dear, what is it?"

"How do you spell *miserable*?"

263. MacLean asked his friend Weaver, "What kind of flower is that in your buttonhole?"

"It's a chrysanthemum," answered Weaver.

"It looks like a rose to me," said MacLean.

"Nope. It's a chrysanthemum," insisted Weaver.

"Spell it," demanded MacLean.

"K-r-i-s-; no, it's k-h-r-y-i; no, it's got to be C-r-i-s-s- . . . . By gosh, you're right, it *is* a rose."

A Logical Barrier

264. Logic is a splendid thing, but perhaps it can be carried to extremes. For example, a New England farmer was building a wall ("Something there is that doesn't love a wall—" Robert Frost) with rocks from his field. He built it twice as wide as it was high. A stranger asked him why he did that.

"Well," he said, "this way, if the wind blows it over, it will be twice as high as it is wide."

Put Yourself in My Shoes

265. A baseball team was doing terribly. Nobody seemed to be able to hit the ball. Finally, the angry coach ordered a special batting-practice session. He grabbed a bat, went up to the plate, and shouted to the pitcher, "Okay, Eddie, throw me some tough ones!"

Unfortunately, the coach was in bad shape and out of practice. He swung at six or seven pitches and missed them all. Then he threw his bat aside and glared at the players.

"All right, you guys, did you see that?" he growled. "That's what you all have been doing. Now learn the lesson and get in there and start slugging!"

266. An older woman's car stalled at a traffic light. She tried and tried, but she couldn't get it to start. Meanwhile, a man in a car behind her was very persistently blowing his horn. Finally, the woman got out and said to the honker, "Look. I can't start my car. Why don't you go see if you can start it, and I'll stay here and lean on your horn?"

Flights of Fancy

When it comes to dealing with problems, it's too bad we aren't all Einsteins.

267. Albert Einstein (1879-1955), after he came to America in 1933, was a professor at the Institute for Advanced Study in Princeton. In the course of his work, he had to sit through quite a few dull academic meetings. A colleague said to him, "Einstein, you must be terribly bored by all this."

"Oh, no," replied the great theoretical physicist. "At times like these, I just retire to the back of my mind, and there I am happy."

10

Signs of Life—II

If you've forgotten what the title of this chapter means, look back at chapter 3: "Signs of Life—I."

Two Signs from Paradise

268. One of the bits of paradise in this world are the Isles of Scilly (*not* the Scilly Isles) in the Gulf Stream off Land's End, the southwest part of Great Britain. Here semitropical gardens grow, and as my wife and I strolled through one of them we saw this sign posted:

> The kiss of the sun for pardon,
> The song of the birds for mirth,
> One is nearer to God in a garden
> Than anywhere else on earth.

Another sign, so old as to be not entirely legible, states to visitors a number of prohibitions. At the very bottom it reads ". . . and to abstain from picking flowers or from scribbling nonsense and such like small nuisances. Enter then, if it so please you, and welcome."

Danger Signs

269. Some joker—or was he serious?—put up some signs along a two-lane road in western Pennsylvania, just outside of a town. The first sign, in bold red letters, read: DANGER AHEAD! A second sign, a short distance beyond in even bolder letters, said: WARNING! DANGER AHEAD!! And then, for no apparent reason, as the road entered the town, there was a third and final sign in green letters: RESUME COMPOSURE. THANK YOU!

Query: Is this the story of life?

270. A young, eager looking executive, very much the take-charge type, got up to go to the rest room on a 747. All the men's rooms were occupied, so he stood in the aisle waiting. The flight attendant noticed him and suggested that he use the ladies room, but she explicitly warned him not to touch the buttons on the left-hand panel.

As he was relieving himself, he couldn't help wondering what those four buttons were all about. Curiosity got the best of him and he pushed the one beside the letters WW. Instantly he felt an unexpectedly delightful flow of warm water cascading over his rear end and genitals. That was so nice that he pushed the second button, marked HA. Warm air flowed out and pleasantly dried him. He could not resist the third button labeled TP. Deliciously fragrant talcum powder caressed his lower parts. By this time he was very envious of the special treatment provided for the ladies and could not contain himself until he tried the fourth button marked TR.

When he awoke in a hospital in the city of his destination, a nurse was standing beside his bed. He asked her, "What happened?"

She replied, "You pushed the button marked TR—Tampon Remover. Your penis is under your pillow."

271. Here, as a lead-in to the next chapter, are some signs I have observed in government offices.

- Don't speak too much hot air. Remember: the average cow belches 35 cubic feet of gas each day.

- Bureaucracy is the art of making the possible impossible.
- When down in the mouth, remember Jonah. He came out all right.—Thomas Edison
- In an I.R.S. office: America is the land of untold wealth.

11

Politics, Government, Bureaucracy, and Law

Too many people have negative thoughts about politics, government, law, and bureaucracy. Politics is simply how we make policy in a democracy (and in a "republicanocracy," too). Whether we like it or not, we *do* need to be governed, and better by law than by dictatorial whim or narrow, grim purpose. As for bureaucracy, most bureaucrats I've met are quite conscientious about doing their duty and creative in their thinking about how to make democracy work.

Politics: The Art of Getting the Vote

272. Harry Nesbitt was a candidate for sheriff. He called on a minister to ask for his support.

"Harry," said the minister, "before I decide, let me ask you a question. Do you enjoy drinking wine and liquor?"

"Well, sir," said Nesbitt, hesitating, "tell me: Is this an inquiry or an invitation?"

273. A politician was running for office. As he walked about town greeting people, kissing babies, and shaking hands, an angry man said to him in a loud voice, "I wouldn't vote for you if you were St. Peter himself."

"That's perfectly OK," replied the politician. "If I were St. Peter you *couldn't* vote for me. You wouldn't be in my district."

274. Heywood Broun (1888-1939), the famous newspaper columnist and critic, was listening with disbelief to a politician at a rally who was giving his own version of the facts.

"How does he get away with it?" whispered a fellow reporter to Broun. "He's murdering the truth."

Broun shook his head in disagreement. "He'll never get close enough to it to do it bodily harm," he said.

275. To get the right people in office, citizens must vote. In 1920, the nineteenth amendment to the Constitution was passed giving women the right to vote—called "woman suffrage." Shortly after this a man—now unknown—was asked, "Do you believe a woman should exercise her franchise?"

"Oh, yes," said his friend. "There's nothing worse than a woman with a flabby franchise."

Donkeys and Elephants

276. Will Rogers (1879-1935), the "cowboy philosopher" and salty political commentator, said, "I'm not a member of an organized political party." Rogers paused to let this sink in and then continued, "I'm a Democrat."

277. A leader of the Democrats frequently showed up at Republican rallies. It seemed strange to the Republicans because he was a well-known Democrat, and finally a Republican asked him, "Why do you come to our gatherings? Do you expect you might get converted to our side?"

"Oh, not at all," replied the Democrat. "It's just that I want to keep my disgust fresh."

Political Characters and Their Memorable Quotes

In politics, thank goodness, there are quite a few people who could be called "characters," and they say some remarkable things.

278. Politics is a complicated and serious mixture of art, science, calculation, and policy-making. An illustration of this is made brilliantly unclear by the following excerpt from a report in the *Daily Camera* of Boulder, Colorado, written over ten years ago:

"The administration has an awful lot of other things in the pipeline, and this has more wiggle room so they just moved it down the totem pole," Baldwin said.

At the same time, Baldwin said that "the White House is as eager as ever to explore for offshore resources. There is no pulling back because of hot-potato factors."

279. Abraham Lincoln (1809–1865) always wanted the plain facts when a proposition was being presented to him. It is said that one day a group of Congressmen were urging him to support a certain action, but they were pretty vague about their information. Lincoln held up his hand, and there was silence. He looked at one of the group and asked, "Mr. Congressman, how many legs would a sheep have if you called its tail a leg?"

"Five," replied the man.

"I guessed you'd say that," Lincoln stated. "Well, you're wrong. The sheep would have four legs. Calling a tail a leg doesn't make it one."

280. Nancy Witcher Longhorne Astor (1879–1965), known as Lady Astor, was the first woman member of the British Parliament. She was a strong character and espoused temperance and women's rights. Even though they were both Conservatives, Lady Astor and Winston Churchill (1874–1965), another strong character, did not get along very well. One day Lady Astor said, "Winston, if you were my husband, I'd put poison in your tea."

Churchill replied, "If I were your husband, Nancy, I'd drink it."

281. Moshe Dayan (1915–1981), the Israeli leader who was Defense Minister of Israel in the 1967 Six-Day War and served his nation in many other capacities, was asked, when he took a controversial position, "But what will people say about you after death?"

Dayan replied, "I'll never know. That's the point of being dead."

282. David Lloyd George (1863-1945), the famous Liberal British statesman, who served in Parliament for fifty-five years and whose term as prime minister (1916-1922) included World War I, was a rather small man. When someone introduced him to a meeting by remarking, "I expected to find Mr. Lloyd George a big man in every sense," Lloyd George replied, "In North Wales, from where I come, we measure a man from his chin up. Here, you evidently measure him from his chin down."

283. A few years ago, in Washington, the British ambassador was telephoned by a local TV station.

"Ambassador," said the caller, "what would you like for Christmas?"

"I shouldn't dream of accepting anything."

"Seriously, we would like to know and don't be stuffy. You have after all been very kind to us during the year."

"Oh, well, if you absolutely insist, I would like a small box of crystallized fruits."

He thought no more about it until Christmas Eve when he switched on the TV and heard the announcer say:

We have had a little Christmas survey all of our own. We asked three visiting ambassadors what they would like for Christmas. The French Ambassador said: "Peace on earth, a great interest in human literature and understanding, and an end to war and strife." Then we asked the German Ambassador, and he said: "A great upsurge in international trade, ensuring growth and prosperity, particularly in the underdeveloped countries. That is what I wish for Christmas." And then we asked the British Ambassador, and he said he would like "a small box of crystallized fruits."

284. One can get a little cynical about politics, government, and even business, not to mention religion and charities. But cynicism has elements of truth in it, and so I quote—from sources unknown—two thought-provoking sentences:

- Organizations exist for the painless extinction of the ideals which gave them birth.

- There is a time in the history of any institution when the institution itself becomes more important than the ideals for which it was founded.

But, please, don't let these thoughts make you cynical. Instead, let them encourage you to keep the ideals alive, wherever you work and whatever you do.

Before we move on from politics to government, consider the political aspects of this weighty exchange of correspondence between an arboretum and a zoo.

285. Philadelphia, like all cities, has its problems, and one of them is the overpopulation of deer, which eat up people's gardens, trees, and shrubs. Here is a proposal from one famous Philadelphia institution, The Morris Arboretum, located in an exclusive section of the city, Chestnut Hill, to "America's oldest zoo"—and certainly one of its best. It was published in *The Philadelphia Inquirer*.

Dec. 15, 1989

Mr. William Donaldson
Philadelphia Zoo
34th and Girard Avenue
Philadelphia, Pa. 19122

In a recent meeting with the officers of the Pennsylvania Game Commission, I was advised that lion urine was a particularly effective deterrent to Pennsylvania deer. No one was sure exactly why this was the case, since no one could quite remember when the last time a Pennsylvania deer had seen a lion. Nevertheless, these "curators" of our state wildlife were quite certain of the virtue of lion urine in this regard.

Since the Morris Arboretum is being severely damaged

by the explosion in the deer population, I did not want to leave any recommendation untested, or, in this case, any stone or bush unanointed with lion urine, if that is what it is going to take to solve our problem. And since you are the "keeper" of the only lions in the area, I thought perhaps you would be willing to provide some assistance.

My hope is that you would allow someone experienced in such matter to catheterize your lions so that we may have a reliable supply of this precious feline fluid. . . . I imagine that lions produce a pretty substantial quantity but given the rate at which the deer population is growing I suspect that we will need all you can provide.

To accommodate such production, I thought perhaps we could lay a pipeline between the zoo and the arboretum. With this new public utility neither of us would be inconvenienced by the necessity of transporting this liquid gold to Chestnut Hill. . . .

Of course, if catheterizing lions and laying a pipeline is not feasible, perhaps you'd be willing to loan us a few lions. We could walk them around the perimeter of the arboretum to mark the boundary of our property. I know you have a program to "adopt an animal" but have you ever considered "leasing a lion"? Who knows, it could be a way of offsetting recent losses in city funding. But then it occurs to me that you may have other plans for your lion urine!

I look forward to your earliest response to my appeal, and take this opportunity to wish you and your staff happy holidays and best wishes for the next decade. You are an inspiration to us all.

Sincerely,

William M. Klein, Director
Morris Arboretum of the
University of Pennsylvania

A couple of weeks later, *The Inquirer* published Donaldson's reply:

William M. Klein, Ph.D.
Director, Morris Arboretum of the
University of Pennsylvania
9414 Meadowbrook Ave.
Philadelphia, Pa. 19118

Dear Bill:

While it was unclear from your letter of December 15, 1989, if you wanted urine from African lions or mountain lions to use in your attempt to protect the arboretum from the deprivations of excessive deer populations, I did consult with both species here at the zoo.

Hercules, who is our male mountain lion, showed the most enthusiasm for your project and suggested he would be willing to spend Mondays, Wednesdays and Fridays at the aboretum and Tuesdays and Thursdays at the Schuylkill Valley Nature Center. He would, however, require copius quantities of beer and one of your gardeners now and again if he is to do his best.

As a city-owned, if not supported, institution we felt we had to offer the services of our lions to the city before offering to help you. We found however that the city has an excessive supply of urine in City Hall and did not show much interest in augmenting that supply.

When I was discussing this problem with our lions, George, who is a patriarch of our Siberian tiger group, overheard me telling them that the carnivore rations may be cut back due to the unwillingness of the city to accept their responsibility to partially fund the operation of the zoo, and volunteered to visit the City Finance Department and some members of City Council.

Tempted as I was to take George up on his offer, my concern for his health, knowing as I do the lack of good taste on the part of some of these officials, made me decline his offer. Hercules and I are both waiting for a reply to our offer, but in the meantime, I realized the potential the zoo has for earning income by renting out animals for various purposes. We have identified a number of these potential projects ranging from gorillas as professional wrestlers to elephants as debt collectors. We have even had a request to rent two of our vultures, which we had to turn down since I was afraid that they would spend most of their time circling City Hall.

Sincerely,

William V. Donaldson

Government

Probably governments work best if the people feel in touch with the head of the government and are familiar with his or her place of residence, whether it be Number 10 Downing Street or the White House. In the days before TV, this wasn't easy for the resident.

286. Up until Theodore Roosevelt's time (he was President from 1901 to 1909), the residence of the President was called The President's House. It was considered to belong to the people, and anybody could come in—in theory, at least. When Charles Dickens (1812-1870) visited America, he walked up to the House and "thrice rang the bell, which nobody answered." So he walked in.

When Thomas Jefferson (1743-1826) was President (1801-1809), he started the custom of hosting an open house on New Year's Day, and this continued until Herbert Hoover's presidency (1929-1933). It had its problems. On January 1, 1902, Theodore Roosevelt shook hands with some 8,100 callers. It was tough on the Chief Executive's right hand!

Well, Abraham Lincoln (President, 1861-1865) had promised to sign the Emancipation Proclamation on January 1, 1863. But he moaned, "I have been shaking hands since nine o'clock this morning, and my right arm is almost paralyzed." He wanted to show a firm hand for his most famous signing—and, somehow, he managed to do so!

287. How does the U.S. government sound or look to people not in it? A Soviet official recently spent an afternoon observing the U.S. House of Representatives in action. After an hour or so, he asked the person sitting next to him, "How do you stop them from talking?"

288. In the pressroom of Michigan's house of representatives, reporters have covered most of one wall with gems of English spoken by Michigan's legislators. Here are some samples (and I advise a visit to the pressroom for further delights):

POLITICS, GOVERNMENT, BUREAUCRACY, AND LAW

- Now we've got them right where they want us.
- This bill goes to the very heart of the moral fiber of human anatomy.
- Let's violate the law one more year.
- There comes a time to put principle aside and do what's right.
- Before I give you the benefit of my remarks, I'd like to know what we're talking about.

289. Peter Finley Dunne (1867–1936), the Chicago journalist, wrote a series of books featuring Mr. Dooley, an Irish saloon keeper who was a great and humorous critic of events and politics. He had this to say about the vice-presidency:

It's sthrange about th' vice-prisidincy. Th' prisidincy is th' highest office in th' gift iv th' people. Th' vice-prisidincy is th' next highest an' th' lowest. It isn't a crime exactly. Ye can't be sint to jail f'r it, but it's kind iv a disgrace. It's like writin' anonymous letters. At a convintion nearly all th' dillygates lave as soon as they've nommynated th' prisidint f'r fear wan iv thim will be nommynated f'r vice-prisidint.

Bureaucracy

290. A farmhand, Kent, was amazingly expert with a whip. Occasionally, when the farm owner had guests, he would ask Kent to perform for their entertainment. One afternoon the owner called on Kent to demonstrate his prowess.

"Yes, sir," said Kent happily, and with his whip knocked the blossom off a flower and killed a fly that alighted on the steps. Then one of the guests said, "That's marvelous, Kent. Now how about that hornets' nest up there?"

Kent shook his head, saying, "A blossom is a blossom and a fly is a fly—but a hornets' nest is an organization."

291. Some of the strengths of, and our frustrations about, bureaucracy come from words. In 1978, the Chancellor of the University of London reported four items of verbal statistics. Draw from them what lesson you will.

- The Lord's Prayer has 56 words.
- The Ten Commandments have 297 words.
- The American Declaration of Independence has 300 words.
- The directive of the European Economic Community (EEC) on the import of caramel and caramel products has 26,911 words.

292. To get an accurate count of America's population is impossible. We're a people on the move, a people who don't like to complete forms, and we are sufficiently undereducated to make it impossible for many of us to fill out a government-produced, gobbledegook-infested form. At the very end of the 1990 census, the "enumerators" used a "Questionnaire Misdelivery Record Nonresponse Follow-Up" (QMRNFU).

In the 1980 census, computers were "instructed" to reject all people aged 112 or over. (You must die before this!) But, said a Population Projectioning Specialist, "we had no requirement that children shouldn't be over 100," so, he said, "You'd look and find two 112-year-old parents with their 109-year-old child." Long live America!

Meanwhile, it's easier, perhaps, to count the stars in the universe. At least they're there, and they have not yet expressed an unwillingness to be counted.

293. If you have any doubts about whether you or your spouse is dead, and what your financial prospects may be, perhaps these words from the Internal Revenue Service's Publication #590 concerning Individual Retirement Accounts (IRAs) will help you:

If your life expectancy, or that of your spouse, is refigured annually and either of you dies, the remaining life expectancy of the one who died is reduced to zero the year after death.

294. Perhaps U.S. and U.S.S.R. bureaucracy have a good deal in common. In Moscow, a well-placed bureaucrat was granted a permit to buy a railroad ticket without having to stand in line. So he went to the station and waved his permit. The ticket agent called, "Get in that line over there."

"But," the bureaucrat protested, "this permit lets me buy a ticket without standing in line."

"Yes, yes," said the agent, "and that is the line for people who don't have to stand in line."

295. A delightful man, Dr. James Boren, is President and Founder of the International Association of Professional Bureaucrats, which has branches in 38 countries—and two in Moscow (as of April 1990).* The INTRAPROBU has three principles of dynamic inaction:

> When in charge, ponder.
> When in trouble, delegate.
> When in doubt, mumble.†

296. Does bureaucracy affect the medical profession, in or out of government? My son-in-law, Larry Weisberg, M.D., a renologist, married to our daughter Becky Johnson, M.D., a pediatrician (the Kids and Kidneys Couple!), had the following letter published in the July 5, 1990, *New England Journal of Medicine*. Receivers of various appeals and proposals should appreciate it.

SALUTATIONS TO A "REGULATED
MEDICAL WASTE GENERATOR"

My dearest Editor:

A recent letter I received from the New Jersey Department of Environmental Protection, Division of Solid Waste Management, Bureau of Special Waste Planning, addressed

---

*The INTRAPROBU has a Russian affiliate: The Soviet Academy of Bureaucratic Arts (SOVACOBA).

†Should you want to be in touch with this deadly humorous, lively serious organization, write to Dr. James H. Boren, President, International Association of Professional Bureaucrats, National Press Building, Washington, DC 20045.

to "Dear Regulated Medical Waste Generator," has prompted me to consider my feelings about the various ways I am greeted. I am happy with "Dear Larry," "Dear Lawrence," "Dear Dr. Weisberg," or "Dear Mr. Weisberg." I don't mind "Dear Doctor" or "Dear Sir," as long as the letter is not from a member of my family. I have come to accept "Dear Friend" from fund-raisers I don't know, and "Dear Provider" from health insurers. I can even understand a computer I've never met addressing me as "Dear Miss Weisberg" (although I prefer "Ms."). But I don't think I shall ever come to terms with "Dear Regulated Medical Waste Generator." What really disappoints me is the absence of a corresponding intimate closing, like "We miss you. Please write soon. Love, NJDEP, DSWM, BSWP."

With warmest personal regards,

Lawrence S. Weisberg, M.D.
Cooper Hospital/University Medical Center
Camden, NJ 08103

297. A Philadelphia friend of mine, Benjamin E. DeRoy, recently suffered a major ordeal in a hospital—which is supposed to *cure* people! Here is his blow-by-blow report:

MIDNIGHT RUDE AWAKENING IN THE HOSPITAL

9:30 p.m. I lie on my hospital bed trying to fall asleep, despite my surgical wounds, my conscience, my upset stomach, noise in the halls and a hard pillow.

11:00 p.m. I finally fall into the most blessed sleep of the century.

12:30 a.m. A flashlight shining in my eyes slowly, painfully awakens me to this world of agony. A thermometer is thrust into my mouth, and a blood pressure cuff is put on my arm.

3:45 a.m. I fall alseep again.

4:25 a.m. You guessed it!—another awakening.

I had read Norman Cousins' story of stopping all unwelcome blood predators, pill bearers, temperature takers, etc. at the threshold of his closed hospital room door. I tried the same thing—but without his clout, as the following sequence of events proves:

1. Sign on my door:
VICIOUS DOG INSIDE.
ABANDON YE ALL HOPE WHO ENTER HERE TO AWAKEN PRINCE CHARMING WHILE HE SLEEPS. COME BACK IN THE MORNING AT 10:00 O'CLOCK FOR LOLLIPOPS AND ENTERTAINMENT.

2. Whispered agitated female voices outside the door—"All I did was . . ." "Who is he?" "What do we do now?"—Then a voice of authority: "We ignore this note! Now get back to work."

3. I protest to the nurse the next morning. This is like trying to change the mind of a traffic cop writing a ticket for speeding.

4. I protest to the head nurse. This is like trying to move the Rock of Gibraltar.

5. I protest to a medical student. This is not part of her curriculum, authority, or responsibility.

6. I protest to an intern. His responsibility, duty, and authority are to discourage all such rebellion on the part of the suffering public.

7. I protest to a hospital resident. She is amused by my naïveté in thinking I can change a hospital policy dating back to Florence Nightingale and the Civil War.

8. I protest to my doctor. Great sympathy, but long explanation and justification of system. I tell him to send me no more bills until I get my sleeping privileges restored.

9. Sign on my door:
WANTED:
PHYSICIAN OR HOSPITAL ADMINISTRATOR WITH AUTHORITY TO CHANGE HOSPITAL RULES. WILL PAY HANDSOMELY ON DELIVERY OF SERVICE.

10. Delegation at my bedside. Division Hospital Administrator, Chief of Surgery, Head of Public Relations, and secretary, who carries a heavy hospital rulebook, tape recorder, and stenographer's notebook. After listening to them defend the system for 15 minutes, I hand them the following note:

> To Whom It May Concern:
> I pay $753 a day for this expensive hotel and rest cure. As long as my sleep is disturbed I shall pay only $417 a day for services rendered here. My rest cure will be deferred until I return home, and therefore I will *not* pay the hospital for it.

11. Letter from the President of the Hospital with "EXCEPTIONAL PRIVILEGES" pocket plastic card (similar to 100,000 mile flight card from an airline, or Platinum Card from American Express), and a plastic sign for my hospital room door saying:

> EXCEPTIONAL PATIENT: SEE HOSPITAL
> RULEBOOK PAGE 732, RULE 41579.

Letter advises me to please enjoy my privileges *quietly* so as to avoid a general uprising, which would disturb the calm and peaceful atmosphere in the hospital. Letter warns me that any other course of mine could start a public revolution, which would then require hiring an additional Vice-President to handle the crisis and its aftermath, thus raising the cost of medical care.

12. Enclosed in the letter is a small sealed envelope with a message written on it, evidently by a secretary: "Please do not open in hospital." The note inside says:

> "Keep it up, brave sir! The American Revolution freed us from British rule and rules but *not* from hospital rules.
> P.S. This note is personal, confidential and deniable."

Law

We are generally not governed by a "government under law." Most laws are useful, perhaps even those that bring people to the point of death.

298. A man was about to be hanged. The sheriff asked him, "Are there any last words you would like to say?"

The man thought a moment and then said, "Yes, sheriff. This certainly is going to be a lesson to me."

299. Criminals can sometimes be especially clever. G. K. Chesterton (1874–1936), the prolific conservative author and Catholic apologist, tells of a bandit who was captured by the King's troopers. The king was fond of riddles, and put this one to the bandit: "You may make one statement. If you tell the truth, you will be shot. If you lie, you will be hanged."

The bandit confused everybody, and perhaps got off, by replying, "I am going to be hanged."

300. Carl Hunsicker was a witness at a trial. The judge was examining him, as follows:

Judge: "Did you *see* that the shot was fired?"
Hunsicker: "No, your honor, I only heard it."
Judge: "Aha! I hereby state this is pure hearsay. It is not admissible as evidence."

Hunsicker left the witness stand and, with his back turned to the judge, laughed loudly.

Judge: "Come back here, Mr. Hunsicker. You may not laugh at me. I shall hold you in contempt of court."
Hunsicker: "Did you see me laugh?"
Judge: "No, but I heard you."
Hunsicker: "According to your rules, Judge, that's inadmissible evidence."

301. During the trial, a lawyer went on and on presenting his case. He had far from finished when he noticed the judge yawning quite openly. The lawyer said, "I hope I am not unduly trespassing on the time of this court."

The judge replied, "There is a difference between trespassing on time and encroaching on eternity."

12

Speakers and Their Speaking

Brevity Is the Soul of Wit

Since speakers very often are not brief, I have decided to make this chapter brief. We'll begin with five stories about brevity, enforced or otherwise.

> **302.** An isolated but civilized and cultured tribe in sub-Saharan Africa has a method for avoiding overly long speeches, which they consider are injurious to both the speaker and the audience. The custom is that the speaker must stand on one leg while addressing his audience. As soon as his second foot touches the ground, he must stop.

> **303.** Whenever I speak to a group, I state well in advance that if the person who introduces me takes more than three minutes, I'll double my fee. It usually works!
>
> Apparently, Thomas Alva Edison (1847–1931) had problems with long introductions. At a dinner, the master of ceremonies went on and on about Edison, and especially his invention of the "talking machine," as record players were then called. After the introduction, Edison arose and said, "I thank the gentleman for his kind remarks, but I must insist upon a correction. God invented the talking machine. I only invented the first one that can be shut off."

304. We all know the expression "hop, skip, and jump," although I've no idea where it came from. It was ingeniously used by a man who described the ideal speaker as one "who hops to the platform, skips his introduction, and jumps to his conclusion."

305. A long-winded speaker was extolling the virtues of Yale. At great length, he explained the Y stands for Youth; A for Appreciation of the great offerings of the university; L for Loyalty, a trait that ennobles and improves people; and (after he had been speaking for nearly an hour) E for Excellence and Efficiency.

A member of the audience whispered to his neighbor, "At least we can be thankful that he didn't attend Massachusetts Institute of Technology!"

306. A speaker realized that he'd gone on too long, and he concluded, "I'm sorry if I spoke too long. You see, I forgot my watch, and there isn't a clock anywhere—"

"But there's a calendar on the wall right next to you," a voice from a dark corner of the auditorium yelled out.

307. And how should you conduct yourself if brevity does not prevail? The prestigious British medical journal *Lancet* gives this excellent advice about a common human problem, that of how to sleep respectfully and inconspicuously during long, dull speaches:

The head should rest on a tripod formed of the trunk and of the arms firmly placed on the table. The head should be placed in the hands in a slightly flexed position to allow the tongue to fall forward and prevent stertorous breathing. The fingers should be outstretched over the face and eyes, pressing the skin of the forehead upwards to wrinkle it. This gives an appearance of deep concentration.

The Techniques of Oratory

These days, except perhaps in churches (see chapter 14, "Religion, In and Out of Church"), we don't have many speakers who are orators.

308. Do you want to be an orator, or do you admire orators? Don't answer before you consider the following:

A man met an old friend whom he hadn't seen in a long time. His friend was very well dressed and so the man asked him, "You look very elegant. How have you become so prosperous?"

The friend replied, "I've got a profession."

"And what is it?" asked the friend.

"I'm an orator," was the reply.

"I see," said the man. "And what's your definition of an orator?"

"I'll tell you," said the orator. "If you ask an ordinary person what two plus two is, he'll say 'Four.' But we orators would say, 'When in the course of human events it becomes necessary to take the numeral of the second denomination and add it to the figure two, I say to you—and I say it without fear of successful contradiction—that the result is invariably four!'"

309. During the discussion period after his lecture, someone asked a famous speaker, "You've given us a wonderful talk. But tell me, do you have any special formula for success?"

"Well, yes," said the speaker, "it is this: In promulgating your esoteric cogitations and articulating superficial, sentimental, and psychological observations, beware of platitudinous ponderosity. Let your extemporaneous decantations and unpremeditated expatiations have intelligibility and veracious veracity without rodomontade and thrasonical bombast. Sedulously avoid all polysyllabic profundity, pusillanimous vacuity, pestiferous profanity and similar trangressions."

Then he paused, smiled, and stated, "What I mean is: talk simply, naturally, and don't use big words."

310. Sometimes speakers unintentionally communicate the exact opposite of what they mean. A school graduate was talking with a classmate at his tenth reunion. "Do you remember the commencement speaker we had?" he asked.

"Yeah, vaguely," replied the classmate.

"Well," said the first man, "I recall one thing . The speaker said to us: 'If there's one thing I want you to remember out of all the things I have told you, it is this!' And there was a dramatic pause. Well, I've always remembered what I just quoted, but I've completely forgotten what the 'this!' was."

311. People often enjoy speeches, but they like to have an idea of how long they will be. I solve this problem by telling the audience, right at the beginning, how long I will talk—and then stopping two minutes early. But have you noticed that there are three other categories of speakers?

- Those who put down on the lectern each page as they read it. That enables the audience to keep track.

- Those who cheat the audience by putting each page under the others, so the pile stays the same size.

- Those, and they are the worst, who put down each page as in the first category, but then pick up the whole batch and read off the other side.

Rising and Falling to the Occasion

312. At the last moment, just before the meeting was to begin, someone rushed up to the chairman of a large meeting to tell him that the flight of the celebrated humorist who was to be the speaker was delayed by bad weather and that he couldn't make it.

Quickly, and quietly, the chairman persuaded two members of the audience, known locally, to substitute. Then he announced, "Ladies and gentlemen, I'm very sorry that the great national wit we were to hear this evening cannot make it. So, at the last minute I have secured the services of two half-wits to take his place."

313. School heads, especially very able ones, often receive extremely challenging requests. This was true of Betty Hall, headmistress of Concord Academy during the fifties and sixties. She was known for her eloquent and humorous "chapels," weekly talks given to students in the school chapel. The following note was written by a Concord Academy student: "Dear Miss Hall: Could you talk about revolutions on Thursday, and on Monday could you talk about life?"

314. A speaker came home very discouraged because he had worked hard on his speech and thought he had delivered it well. He said to his wife: "The applause sounded like a caterpillar in slippers romping across a Persian carpet."

Brutally Honest

315. Sinclair Lewis (1885-1951), the great American novelist, was the author of *Main Street, Babbitt, It Can't Happen Here,* and some nineteen other novels. He was born in Sauk Centre, Minnesota, and went to Yale. Toward the end of his life, he went back to New Haven for a class reunion and was hailed and flattered by his classmates. Many speakers said that at Yale they'd recognized his genius and had enjoyed helping him. When Lewis himself was called upon to speak, he said, according to a classmate's memory:

When I came to Yale I was a freckle-faced, red-haired, gangling greenhorn from a small town in Minnesota, and all of you either ignored me or high-hatted me. Now that I've been lucky enough to achieve a little notoriety, you've changed your tune and are trying to horn in on the act. You were not my friends then, and you're not my friends now. And as far as I'm concerned, you can all go to hell.

13

Smart Kid Answers—II

316. A teacher of a rather rowdy sixth-grade class was called out of the classroom for a few minutes. When she returned, she found all the pupils sitting quietly at their desks.

"My goodness!" she said. "What's the explanation for this?"

One of the class wise guys raised his hand and sarcastically replied, "Don't you remember, Teacher? A couple of days ago you told us that if you left the room and came back and found us all sitting still, you'd drop dead."

317. Teaching is a risky business, even the teaching of grammar. For example, Miss Sullivan asked her class, "What tense is 'I am beautiful'?"

Hands were raised and she called on Mike, who answered, "Past."

318. A very bright, honest young girl was told by her mother: "Jenny, I'd just love it if you'd spend as much time on your homework as you do in making up elaborate excuses."

Jenny replied, "Miss Churchill says it's good for young minds to exercise their imaginations."

319. A young boy, who was new in the neighborhood and wanted to find some friends, rang the doorbell of a nearby house one Saturday. When a woman came to the door, the boy said, "May I speak to the kid of the house?"

320. A Sunday-school teacher was explaining the Golden Rule to her class. After reading from the Bible—"As ye would men do unto you, do ye also unto them likewise."—the teacher asked about this turn-the-other-cheek idea: "Now, Gordon, supposing a boy hit you?"

Gordon, not a Bible devotee, asked, "How big a boy are you supposing."

Oh, the practicality of youth!

321. A small boy sitting in church with his father suddenly felt sick to his stomach. "Dad," he said, "I think I have to throw up."

His father whispered, "Well then go quickly to the restroom."

The boy came back sooner than expected. His father asked, "Are you all right now?"

"It worked out OK, Dad. I didn't have to go very far. Right by the door there's a box that says 'FOR THE SICK.'"

322. Sometimes little children have plain answers to deep questions. Our daughter is a Quaker married to a Jew. Her two children go to Day Care at the local Jewish Center. There they have a good time and learn quite a lot about Jewish practices and thought.

One evening I was alone with granddaughter Molly, then almost four years old. She calls me Gramps. On the spur of the moment I decided to ask her a deep question.

Gramps: "Molly, where is God?"

Molly (after a long, thoughtful pause): "I don't know."

Gramps: "Well, what is God?"

Molly (in a quiet but definite voice): "Something Jewish."

323. The pastor of a small fundamentalist church, a diligent though perhaps not very inspiring man, always asked children the same questions in the same order when he visited homes in the parish: "What's your name? How old are you? Did you say your prayers? What will happen to you if you don't say your prayers?"

One very careful mother made her little boy practice the answers. When the pastor called, he went up to the boy and before he had a chance to open his mouth the boy rattled off: "Calvin Ericson; five; yes; go to hell."

324. Little Margarita was taken to church for the first time. Afterward, the minister asked, "Margarita, how did you like the service?"

"Well," she said thoughtfully, "I thought the church was beautiful and the music was very nice—but your commercial was too long."

Lesson: If you want the truth, ask a little child!

14

Religion, In and Out of Church

So: do you want the truth about religion? You've just read what a little child said about sermons in church. Let's, for a moment, go beyond sermons to prayer. Is prayer a way to get to, or submit yourself to, truth?

Prayer

325. Sometimes children have amazing faith in the efficacy of prayer. Celeste was saying her prayers as her mother listened. "Oh, please, God, make Boston the capital of Vermont."

"Celeste," exclaimed her mother, "why in the world did you say that?"

"Mom," said Celeste, "I wrote that on my geography test today, and I want it to be correct."

326. A toddler was beginning to get noisy during the sermon of a Catholic church service. The child's mother picked up her youngster and began to carry him out when the priest stopped the sermon and addressed the woman: "*Please* don't take your child out. He needs to be here. This is where he'll hear about God."

Then he said to the congregation, "Now let's all be very quiet and just listen." They were, until all that could be heard was the babbling of a few babies. Then the priest said, "You know, this is what our prayers sound like to God."

327. Michelangelo Buonarroti (1475-1564) was commissioned by Pope Julius II (1443-1513) to paint the ceiling of the Sistine Chapel in the Vatican with scenes from the Bible. He worked on the project from 1508-1512, four years. It was rumored that Michelangelo, while quietly at work far above the altar, noticed a certain woman coming in day after day to pray. After a while, Michelangelo whispered loudly, "This is Jesus speaking." Because of the acoustics, the source of the whisper was impossible to identify. Michelangelo kept saying, "This is Jesus speaking," until one day the woman got annoyed and while still on her knees, shouted, "Be quiet! I'm talking to your mom."

328. It was a terribly hot and humid day, and the family had a number of guests to dinner. The mother of the family said to her young son, "Sidney, will you please say grace before we start the meal?"

"But, Mom," said Sidney, "I don't know what to say."

"Oh, just say what you've heard me say," replied Mom.

So everyone bowed their heads and Sidney intoned, "Oh, Lord, why did I invite these people here on a sweltering day like this?"

Adapting the Bible to Real Life

How realistic, plausible, or useful are the stories in the Bible?

329. Sometimes in this modern age of technology, it's quite hard for children to believe in the classical stories in the Bible. For example, nine-year-old Graham's father asked him what he had learned in Sunday School.

"Well, Dad," said Graham, "it was great. The teacher told us about when God sent Moses behind the enemy line to rescue the Israelites from Egyptian slavery. Well, when they came to the Red Sea, this Moses called for some engineers to build a pontoon bridge. After the Jews had all crossed, they looked back and saw the Egyptian tanks coming. Moses radioed headquarters on his walkie-talkie to send bombers to blow up the bridge and saved the Israelites."

"Wait a minute, Graham," said his father. "Is that really what your teacher told you?"

"Not exactly," Graham admitted, "but if I told it her way, you'd never believe it."

Shall we revise the Holy Scriptures?*

330. Suzie's mother heard her and some friends plotting violent revenge against their neighbor Emily, who apparently had been doing some pretty nasty things. The mother called Suzie to her and said, "Susan, I'm surprised at you. You go to church and know the Golden Rule, and yet it sounds to me as if you girls are going to do to Emily something you wouldn't want done to you."

"Oh, Mom, come on!" exclaimed Suzio. "The Golden Rule is OK for Sunday, but for the rest of the week it's an eye for an eye and a tooth for a tooth."†

331. This is supposed to be a true story, although it has been passed down over a good many years. A fundamentalist bishop from the East visited a small religious college in the Midwest in the 1890s. The president of the college was a young, liberal man who also taught chemistry and physics. The bishop met informally with the faculty and, during the discussion, said, in effect, "The millennium is about to come. Christ will reign on earth. Many signs show it. For example, we have discovered almost everything about nature. Also, all possible major inventions have been made."

The president disagreed strongly, and the bishop was outraged. He said, "Name one major invention that will be made in the next generation."

"Well," said the president, "I feel quite sure that before long people will be able to fly through the air like birds."

---

*Note: The real story is in Exodus 14:5-31.

†From the Book of Exodus 21:24. By the way, the law of an eye for an eye follows shortly after the Ten Commandments (Exodus 20: 3-17) and, as few people realize, is also one of God's commandments. In fact there are over 500 "laws of Moses."

"That's a sinful remark!" the bishop shouted. "Flying is reserved for angels!"

The name of the bishop was Wright and he had two sons, Orville and Wilbur.*

332. Sometimes being a minister doesn't have as many advantages as some clerics might hope, especially when they are confronted by other religious people. For example, a minister was forced by a traffic cop to pull over for speeding. As the cop was making out the ticket, the minister said to him, "Blessed are the merciful, for they shall obtain mercy."

The cop handed the minister the ticket and said, "Go thou and sin no more."

333. A man put this note under the windshield wiper of his car: "I've circled the block for 20 minutes. I'm late for an appointment, and if I don't park here, I'll lose my job. 'Forgive us our trespasses.' "

When he returned, he found a parking ticket and this note: "I've circled the block for 20 years, and if I don't give you a ticket, I'll lose my job. 'Lead us not into temptation.'"

334. We all know the Golden Rule in the Gospel of Luke, 6:31, where Jesus said, "Therefore all things whatsoever that men should do to you, do ye even so unto them"—which has been simplified to: "Do unto others as you would have them do unto you."

One day in church, when the congregation knelt in prayer, they came to the Golden Rule, and an aggressive young kid was heard to say, "Do unto others before they do unto you."

Fair-Weather Friend

335. Since 1968, I've jogged about 27,000 miles with my friend and neighbor Eli Rock. Eli is a Jew; I am

---

*Orville Wright (1871–1948) and Wilbur Wright (1867–1912) made the first power-driven flight near Kitty Hawk, N.C., in 1903.

a Quaker. According to our perhaps somewhat misguided theologies, I, the Quaker, can speak directly with God, while Eli, being a Jew, must work through Moses (born in Egypt in the thirteenth century B.C.).

Eli and I have conducted a quasi-scientific study concerning which of us, Jew or Quaker, can evoke more of God's power to affect the weather. My speculation was that a direct-to-God Quaker could do better than a through-Moses Jew. However, now we have definitely determined that Eli's through-Moses powers are greater than mine. When I jog with Eli it is *much* less likely to rain (or snow) than when I jog alone. And when Eli jogs alone, he seldom gets wet—except through sweat.

We call this phenomenon "The Red Sea Syndrome," and my advice to Quakers (and other like thinkers) is: If you want to jog dry, jog with a Jew!

The Last Accurate Forecast

336. Modern-day weather forecasters are good, but far from perfect. As some believer said, "Probably the last fully accurate weather forecast was when God told Noah there was a 100 percent chance of precipitation."

George Washington on God

337. We've been using the word "God." It might be appropriate to interject here the words of the "father of our country," George Washington (1732–1799):

A reasoning being would lose his [or her?] reason in attempting to account for the great phenomena of nature, had he [she] not a Supreme Being to refer to; and well has it been said that if there had been no God, mankind [humankind?] would have been obliged to imagine one.

Could this possibly mean that George Washington (George Washington, yet!) was in his clearest thinking moments an atheist?!

Walk in the Straight and Narrow Path

How well-behaved can religion help us be? It's an important question, but there are different answers.

> **338.** Mrs. Travis was a delightful, fairly religious woman, who was always seeing the bright side of things, and, even more so, of people.
>
> Two men saw Mrs. Travis walking down the street, and one said to the other, "I bet you can't name anybody whom Mrs. Travis can't say a good word about."
>
> "I'll take you up on that," said the other man. And as Mrs. Travis was about to pass them, he greeted her.
>
> "Good afternoon, Mrs. Travis. May I ask you—what do you think about the Devil?"
>
> "Well," said the lady with a smile, "you'll have to admit he's always on the job."

> **339.** A Catholic priest was talking with the children at a kindergarten in a parochial school. He spoke of Jesus, and of sinners, and of our need for help.
>
> "Who," he asked the children, "has never sinned? I ask you, who of us can say that we are perfect?"
>
> All the children in the class raised their hands.

> **340.** A preacher delivered a good, practical sermon and at the end said, "Now, my brothers and sisters, I saw many of you nodding your heads and even saying 'Amen?' while I was preaching. Well, I think what I've told you is right. Now there are two things you must do: first, believe it; second *behave* it!"

> **341.** When I was principal of Friends' Central School in Philadelphia (1948-52), I was honored to be invited to join the Rotary Club, representing the "business or professional" category Private Schools (now called Independent Schools). As I remember, the Club permitted only one member from each category. More recently, I heard of a creative solution for getting more than one member of a club into the "Religion: Protestant" category. A local Methodist minister filled that category,

and then a Methodist Bishop, a very able man with lots of friends, moved into the area. The Rotary Club met and solved the problem by classifying the minister "Religion: Retail" and the Bishop "Religion: Wholesale."

342. A Roman Catholic priest was showing a Presbyterian minister through a splendid new church. They came to the rectory, where the priests lived. It was magnificent.

"Wow!" said the minister. "This certainly is better than our parsonage!"

"Well," said the priest, "you Protestants have better halves, so I really do think we deserve better quarters."

Death and Afterlife

When human beings consider death, sometimes they become more religious, sometimes not, or sometimes they just avoid the subject.

343. A minister was counseling a woman church member who was having marital problems. He asked the woman, "Does your husband believe in life after death?"

"After death?" exclaimed the woman. "Why he doesn't even believe in life after supper."

344. In 1985–86, my wife and I spent a year in England, a country rich in beautiful churches, large and small. I took some pleasure in walking slowly around the burial grounds reading the inscriptions on tombstones. All of them were sincere, many deeply touching, but I was amazed at how many managed to avoid using the plain word *died*. Here are some of the words and phrases used instead:

> left this life
> fell asleep
> departed this life
> for ever at rest
> entered into rest
> taken by the hand that is divine
> passed to a fuller life
> now reunited

> taken to his Holy Home
> met again on that beautiful shore
> Home with Jesus
> Jesus called her away
> God recalled the precious loan

There was also avoidance of the word *buried*. Instead:
> lies the body
> lyeth the remains
> are deposited the Remains
> lies all that was mortal
> whose remains lie interred
> lies interred the body
> who remains repose

I guess the most vigorous message we read was at Stratford-upon-Avon, where William Shakespeare (1564–1616) is buried. On the gravestone is inscribed:

> Good friend for Jesus sake forebeare,
> To digg the dust enclosed heare.
> Blest be ye man ty spares thes stones,
> And curst be he ty moves my bones.

345. Phillips Brooks (1835–1893), who wrote the hymn "O Little Town of Bethlehem" and was the Episcopal bishop of Massachusetts, had been seriously ill and, to hasten his recovery, refused all visitors—except one, Robert G. Ingersoll (1833–1899), the famous lawyer, orator, and agnostic.

At the start of their visit, Ingersoll asked, "Why do you see me when you refuse to see your friends?"

Bishop Brooks replied, "Well, I feel confident of seeing my friends in the next world, but this may be my last chance of seeing you."

346. A drunk got into a bus and staggered to a seat beside a priest. He sat for a few minutes looking at the priest, who was reading his Bible. Suddenly the drunk shouted, "I'm not going to heaven because there is no heaven!"

The priest ignored this and went on reading the

Holy Scriptures. Then the man bellowed even louder, "I'm not going to heaven because there is no heaven! Now, what do you say, padre?"

The priest replied, "Well, then, go to hell, but for heaven's sake be quiet about it."

347. Friedrich Wilhelm Nietzche (1844-1900) rejected the "slave morality" of Christianity. Driving through the German countryside, someone saw a sign saying: " 'God Is Dead'—Nietzche." Underneath was attached another sign: " 'Nietzche Is Dead'—God."

Theological Conundrums

The scholarly study of the scriptures is difficult, fascinating, and complicated. I know from the experience of writing my book *An Introduction to Jesus of Nazareth: a Book of Information and a Harmony of the Gospels*. So what do people do when faced with hard questions?

348. The Irish bishop James Ussher (1581-1656) was asked, "What was God doing before He created the earth?"

Ussher answered, "He was creating Hell and damnation for people who ask that question."

349. At Boston College, an excellent Roman Catholic institution in Chatham, Mass., a young priest gave a long, clear lecture on theology. He then said, "Are there any questions?"

A student stood up and said, "Father, can you give us documentary proof of the statements you have made about . . . ?" and he listed some subjects.

"I have no proof with me," said the professor, "but I can obtain it easily."

"Well, sir," said the student, "until you produce the evidence, I am going to call you a liar."

The professor paused, stroked his chin, and then replied, "May I please see your parents' marriage certificate?"

The student sat silent and embarrassed while the professor continued, "Until you produce evidence to the contrary I am going to call you an impertinent young bastard."

350. Many Biblical scholars have great difficulty understanding the last book of the Bible, *Revelation*. A young divinity student, John (not a saint, and not divine), had a beloved aunt whom he often called when he was puzzled by his studies. A recent telephone conversation, reportedly, went thus:

John: "Aunt Harriet, what are you doing these days?"

Aunt Harriet: "I'm deeply involved in a Bible study group."

John: "What part of the Bible are you studying?"

Aunt Harriet: "The Book of Revelation."

John: "Oh, Aunt Harriet, at Divinity School we think it's a *very* difficult book."

Aunt Harriet: "Oh, it is, it is. So when we can't understand it, we just explain it to each other."

351. Philosophy and theology are deep, mysterious subjects. At a prestigious university, a philosopher and a theologian were having a deep discussion. The theologian said, "Dr. Cranbrook, I think a philosopher resembles a blind man in a dark room looking for a black cat—which isn't there."

"Perhaps," replied Cranbrook, "but a theologian would have found it."

Unshakable Principles

To judge by the Ten Commandments, God has some strong principles—and so do some people.

352. According to the Bible, Moses led his people—the Israelites—out of Egypt, was in constant touch with God, and was the source of much of the Hebrew Scriptures. But he is best known as the man who received the Ten Commandments directly from God. It is said that he went up Mt. Sinai several times. The first time he received the commandments, he descended and read them to the waiting multitude; but there was so much protest that he had to go back up the mountain and negotiate with God.

At last he came down for the last time and said, "This is it! My people, I have good news and bad news. The good news is that I've got the Commandments down to ten! [Cheers from the crowd.] The bad news is that adultery is still in!"

353. Ammon Hennacy was a farmer in Arizona, but there wasn't much money in farming, so he practiced Christianity on the side. Now Christianity forbids war, so Ammon wouldn't fight or pay his taxes so that other people could buy guns to fight with.

Every April 15th, he picketed the IRS office in Phoenix. On one April 15, a friend came up to him on the IRS office steps in Phoenix and said, "Ammon, why don't you cease and desist? You can't change the world this way."

"Who's trying to change the world?" said Ammon. "I'm just trying to keep the world from changing me."

354. An atheist insomniac who had dyslexia kept waking up at night repeating, "There is no dog."

The Madison Avenue Approach to Religion

I suppose the place where we learn a good deal about holy principles is in church, but how do we get people to attend?

355. In California, a Congregational Church bulletin published this item by the pastor, the Rev. C. W. Kirkpatrick: "This . . . is . . . the . . . way . . . the . . . church . . . sometimes . . . looks . . . to . . . the . . . pastor . . . when . . . he . . . goes . . . into . . . the . . . pulpit."

"Wouldlooklikethisifeverybodybroughtsomebodyelsetochurch."

Another church bulletin board in the East dealt with the same problem thus: "Wanted: men, women, and children to sit in slightly used pews."

356. On a church bulletin board in the Bronx the following was boldly displayed:

SAFETY TIPS

- Do not ride in an auto. They cause 20 percent of all fatal accidents.
- Do not stay at home. Seventeen percent of all accidents happen there.
- Do not walk in the street. Fifteen percent of all accidents happen to pedestrians.
- Do not travel by air, rail, or water. Sixteen percent of all accidents happen during such travel.
- *Do* go to church. Only .001 percent of all accidents happen there.

357. Seen on a church bulletin board while I was walking by:

SUNDAY'S SERMON

What is Hell?
Come early and hear the choir practice.

Mutual Appreciation

358. Mutual appreciation of different religions can start very young. An example is this neighborhood conversation overheard by an adult. It was between two seven-year-olds.

Child 1: "What church do you go to?"

Child 2: "I don't go to church. I go to temple. I'm Jewish."

Child 1: "Jewish? What's that?"

Child 2: "Well, you know, there are Protestants, Catholics, and Jews. But they're all just different ways of voting for God."

I suppose, in a way, this chapter so far has been making fun of religion. But since the noblest subjects can stand being joked about, let's continue.

The Holy Places of Detroit

359. A woman was on a sight-seeing tour of Detroit. Going out Jefferson Avenue, the driver of the bus called out all the places of interest.

"On the right," he announced, "we see the Dodge home."

"John Dodge?" the woman asked.

"No, madam, Horace Dodge."

Continuing on further, he called out: "On the far left corner we have the Ford home."

"Henry?" she suggested.

"No, lady, Edsel."

Still farther out on Jefferson: "On the near-left crossing you will see Christ Church."

"Jesus?" the woman asked with a twinkle. "Or am I wrong again?"

Devils and Angels

360. Mark Twain's famous remark, "Heaven for the climate, Hell for the company," raises the question of what characters are most useful to us in life before we go to H. or H.—or to rot. This poem by R. P. Lister, whose nationality and dates I cannot find, helps answer the question.

THE DEVIL AND THE ANGELS

I have encountered many times
  The Devil in disguise,
My partner in a thousand crimes,
  My lead in many lies.

A useful colleague, a supreme
  Aid in the world's dark ways.
Yet one I hold in no esteem,
  And one I will not praise.

I praise the angels, who, like lambs,
  Are free from fear and doubt,
Who land me in a thousand jams
  And never help me out.

Ecumenical Safari

361. Three clergymen, a Methodist, a Catholic, and an Episcopalian went on a safari together in the wilds of Africa. As they walked through the jungle, suddenly an enormous lion killed all three and then ate them up. A few hours later, in another part of the jungle, the lion had an ecumenical movement.

Jewish Humor

362. I know many Jews, one of the most wonderful being my son-in-law. And I greatly enjoy Jewish humor, even though it may be a bit masochistic. But, as a non-Jewish friend said, "Humor is the flip side of tragedy." Anyway, this point about Jewish humor is so often raised that when one lecturer on the subject was asked, "Is Jewish humor masochistic?" he replied, "No!—and if I hear that question once more I'm going to kill myself."

363. An elderly Jew on a trip was suddenly taken sick and admitted to a Catholic hospital for surgery. The nun who was doing the paperwork asked who would pay the bill.

"Well," said the Jew, "my only living relative is my sister, but she is an old maid who converted to Catholicism and now is a nun."

"Wait a minute!" said the hospital nun. "We nuns are not old maids. We are brides of Christ."

"Oh, fine," smiled the old man. "In that case, send the bill to my brother-in-law."

364. Three Jewish craftsmen were doing repair work on a beautiful Catholic cathedral. The priest asked them to stop work because an important ceremony—the investiture of a nun—was about to commence. One of them asked, "Well, tell us, what is the meaning of this great happening?"

"It is beautiful and holy," replied the priest. "The young woman is giving her life to the Church. She will become a bride of Christ."

"That sounds wonderful," said the craftsman. "May we attend?"

"I don't think it would be proper. It is a sacred Catholic ceremony, and you men are not of the faith."

"Well," smiled the craftsmen, "it should be appropriate. After all, we are relatives of the groom."

The Wages of Sin

365. As a priest was hearing confessions in the church, the janitor was quietly sweeping the floors and dusting the pews. One man came in, entered the confessional, and said, "Oh, Father, I have sinned three times . . ." and he recited his sins. The priest said, "In the name of God, I forgive you. Now if you'll just put five dollars in the contribution box, you may go forth a righteous man."

Soon another man entered and said, "Oh, Father, I have sinned three times," and the same routine occurred.

Then a third man entered and said, "Oh, Father, I have sinned twice."

From the back of the church came the janitor's voice, loud and clear, "Go out and sin again, Brother. We have a special today, three sins for five dollars."

Religious Taboos

366. A Jew, a Hindu, and a lawyer were hiking in the country. As the sun began to set, they realized that they would have to find a place to spend the night. At last they came upon a small inn, but the proprietor said, "I'm sorry. I have only two beds left. One of you will have to sleep in the barn. But it's not bad."

So the three drew lots, and the Jew lost. He went out to the barn, but within ten minutes he was back. "I can't sleep there," he said. "There are pigs in that barn."

So the Hindu unselfishly offered to take his place in the barn. However, soon he was back. "I cannot do it," he said. "I did not realize there were cows in there, and cows are sacred."

So there being no other solution, the lawyer slept in the barn. The next morning his friends asked him how it was. "Fine," he replied. "I spent a long and comfortable night. As soon as I entered the barn, all the cows and pigs left the building."

Monks Are No Fun

367. Religion, as we have seen, can be a humorous subject (Thank God!), and one who knew this was the English humorist Edward Lear (1812-1888), whose *Book of Nonsense* is a classic of wit—especially the limericks—and illustrations. Once after Lear had visited some monks on Mt. Athos, a Greek Orthodox theocratic community from which women and female animals are barred, he wrote:

More pleasing in the sight of the Almighty, I really believe, and more like Jesus Christ intended man to become, is an honest Turk with six wives, or a Jew working hard to feed his little old do' babbies, than these muttering, miserable, mutton-hating, man-avoiding, misogynic, morose and merriment-marring monotoning, many-mule-making, mocking, mournful, minced-fish and marmalade-masticating Monx.

Read it aloud to get the full effect. Also, be sure you realize where Lear's tongue is!

The Trials of Puritan Pets

Sometimes irreverence—or is it irrelevance?—can be shown by a person who is such a stickler for religious principles that he forces even house pets to practice human religious rules and, if they don't, imposes upon the pets the ultimate penalty.

368. In England, just north of Oxford, is the old town of Banbury. Some of its dwellers were Puritans, members of a religious group who, from the seventeenth century on, tried to reform everything, and especially the Church of England. The Church cast them out, but the Puritans continued fervently to apply their principles, as shown by this old saying in verse picked up by a Quaker traveler in the mid-eighteenth century and recited with delight.

> Proud Banbury, poor people,
> Built a church without a steeple.
> As I came through Banbury town
> There I saw a Puritan one
> Hanging of his cat on Monday
> Because it killed a mouse on Sunday.

Sunday School

369. Children, even (or perhaps especially) in Sunday school, can get things a little confused. For example, the teacher asked, "Who can tell us the story of Adam and Eve?"

A child raised her hand and then said, "First of all God created Adam. Then He looked at Adam and thought, 'I think I can do better. I'll try again.' So," said the child, "he created Eve."

370. Young Suzie had been thinking about her life and her father's life, and the fact that her dad kept requiring her to go to Sunday school. Finally, in exasperation, she asked, "Daddy, did you go to Sunday school every week?"

"Of course I did, Suzie," replied Dad.

"Well," reacted Suzie, looking at her father without much admiration, "I bet it won't do me any good either."

Preachers

Religions and churches wouldn't do very well without preachers, and being a preacher is not easy. You and your congregation may "praise the Lord," but you yourself don't always get praised, nor do you always deserve it.

371. A small girl suffered through a sermon during which the preacher shouted very loudly, over and over, to God against sin. After church the girl went up to him and whispered, "Sir, if you got closer to God you wouldn't have to shout so loud."

372. This may be an old story, but I'm sure it's based on fact. A sexton, cleaning up the pulpit after Sunday service, took a peek at the preacher's manuscript. Along the left margin were instructions such as: "Pause here," "Wipe brow here," "Use angry fist gesture," "Look upward."

Near the end was a long paragraph of texts, opposite which the preacher had marked in large capital letters: "ARGUMENT WEAK HERE. YELL LIKE HELL!"

373. A small-town minister in New Hampshire didn't get much of a salary, so he also ran a small farm. One day he saw his hired man sitting idly by the plow while the horses took a needed rest. The minister was displeased. After all, he was paying the man five dollars an hour.

"Eb," he said, "I think it would be a good idea if you carried a pair of shears with you, and you could trim the bushes while the horses rest."

"You're probably right, Reverend," replied Eb. "And I have a suggestion for you. Why not take a bag of potatoes with you into the pulpit and peel them during the hymn singing?"

374. On Easter, a preacher surveyed his packed church, and then started his sermon on this cheerful note: "Since I shall not be seeing many of you again until next Easter, let me take this occasion to wish you a Merry Christmas!"

375. The preacher started his sermon directly and boldly. "Brothers and sisters," he said, "our subject today is 'Liars.' Now, let me ask you a question. How many of you have read the thirty-fifth chapter of Matthew?"

Almost every hand went up.

"Aha!" said the minister. "You are the very people I need to preach to. The Gospel of Matthew has only twenty-eight chapters."

376. The rural Baptist minister preached loudly, "Get your sins washed away!"

One of the congregation dared to interrupt: "I already have, over at the Methodist church."

"Oh, Brother," said the preacher, "you haven't been washed; you've just been dry cleaned."

If it seems like a far cry from religion to money, go quickly to the next chapter.

15

Money and Fund-Raising

Donations

No church could get along without donations, and there are various ways to stimulate people to make them.

> **377.** A minister told the organist how the morning service was to go. Then he said, "After my sermon, I'm going to ask those members who are willing to give $25 or more for new choir robes to stand." He paused and then said, "It may take a few minutes for people to make up their minds, so play some appropriate music while they are considering."
> "All right. I've got just the thing," said the organist.
> After the minister made his appeal, the organist played, full-volume, "The Star-Spangled Banner."*

> **378.** Just before the collection at a large, prosperous church, the pastor announced, "Do not forget, brothers and sisters, that what you are about to give is tax-deductible, cannot be taken with you, and is, according to the Holy Bible, the root of all evil."

> **379.** The Reverend Dominic received a call from an Internal Revenue Service man, who said, "Father, your member Jacob Watkins states on his tax return that

---

*The results were better than those when a lady sat down on a new-fangled musical toilet seat, and it played the same song!

he gave $8000 last year to your church. Is that true?"

"I don't have my records here," replied the Reverend. "I'll have to check on it. But, in any case, if he didn't, he will."

Taxes!

380. A Dutchman was describing the red, white, and blue flag of the Netherlands to an American. "It always makes me think of our taxes. When we talk about them, we turn red; when we calculate the amount we owe, we turn white; and when we pay them we turn blue."

"Just like us!" exclaimed the American, "except that in the U.S.A. we see stars, too."

Precocious Entrepreneurs

381. Sometimes even the President of the United States is forced to see himself in perspective. This happened to Herbert Hoover (1874-1964; President 1928-32), when a small boy asked him for an autograph. The ex-President liked bold youngsters and signed the boy's card. The boy then asked, "Mr. President, would you mind signing four more times?"

"Hmm? Why do you want four more?"

"Well," said the kid, "it takes four Hoovers to get one Babe Ruth." (1895-1948)

382. Bright young Nelson will doubtless make a successful entrepreneur. One day he asked, "Daddy, how much am I worth?"

His father replied, "You're worth a million dollars to me, Son."

"Well," said Nelson, "in that case would you please lend me one dollar on account?"

383. A budding fundraiser, only ten years old, approached a businessman and asked, "Sir, would you like to join our Boys' Club?"

The man handed the boy $5.00 and was given a card reading "Associate Member."

"Well," said the contributor, "as a member, what are my rights and privileges?"

The boy thought for a moment, then replied, "It gives you the right to contribute again next year. And thank you!"

How to Hang on to Your Money

384. Work rules have become so strict that even hold-up men are insecure. A robber shoved a note under a bank teller's window which said, "I've got you covered. Hand over all the money in the cage and don't say a word."

The teller opened the cash drawer and wrote something down. Then he closed the drawer and returned the note to the robber. On the back he had written, "Kindly go to the next window. I'm on my lunch hour."

385. A driver told a tollbooth attendant, "I'm sorry. I only have a twenty."

The attendant smiled and replied, "That's OK, sir. We don't give change on Sundays."

386. The French poet Germain Saint-Foix (1698–1776) had a large income but, perhaps because he was a poet, was always in debt. One day Saint-Foix was in the barber's chair, lathered up, waiting to be shaved. Just then a tradesman entered the shop. It happened that Saint-Foix owed him a large amount of money. When the man recognized the poet, he angrily demanded that he be paid—now! Saint-Foix calmed him down by saying, "Won't you wait for the money until I'm shaved?"

"Certainly," said the creditor, well-pleased at how easy it had been.

"Barber," said Saint-Foix, "you just witnessed this agreement, yes?"

"Of course," said the barber.

Saint-Foix took a towel, wiped off his face, and

happily left the shop. From then on until his death, he wore a beard.

Who says poets aren't practical?

16

Signs of Life—III

The stories in the preceding chapter are about money; those in the next one are about business, one of whose purposes is supposed to be to earn money—also, of course, to make products and provide services. Can you imagine ways the following signs in business offices would help accomplish these purposes?

387.

- Above the entrance to a large office department: Please use your sixth sense: HUMOR
- On an executive's desk: Nobody's perfect. I'm the perfect example.
- On an executive's desk: Truth is a precious commodity and therefore should be used as sparingly as possible.—Mark Twain
- On a secretary's desk: Fact-finding beats fault-finding.
- At a health insurance office: Get our reliable health insurance. Don't make your doctor perform a walletectomy.
- In a mechanics shop: An idealist: One who has both feet firmly planted in the air.
- In an executive's office: Sometimes silence is the best way to yell.
- In a sales conference room: Babe Ruth struck out 1213 times.

- On an office desk in a large business: They don't dare fire me. I'm always too far behind in my work.

- On an office wall: Even moderation ought not to be practiced to excess.

- On the same office wall: One of the greatest labor-saving devices of today is tomorrow.

The next group of signs are a bit more specific, but also about "business."

388.

- In the window of a cleaning shop: QUALITY DRY CLEANERS—Twenty-eight years on the same spot.

- Outside an auto muffler shop: No appointment necessary. We hear you coming.

- Beside a dentist's office: Patient parking only. All others will be painfully extracted.

- Over a barn door: Agriculture is something like farming, only farming is doing it.

- On a New Hampshire septic tank truck: You make it, we take it. We rush so you can flush. You dump it, we pump it. The underside of life; get the truth from us.

- At the top of a stepladder in Ireland: Proceed no further.

17

Business

America is the land of opportunity, and one of the big opportunities is to go into business. But opportunities often involve problems.

Business Setbacks

389. A tale published some years ago by the *ERA Journal of the Eastern Region of the Royal Institute of British Architects* aptly illustrates how a complicated job involving architecture and construction can often turn out to be much more difficult than anticipated. It is titled "Noah Way."

And the Lord said unto Noah: "Where is the ark which I have commanded thee to build?"

And Noah said unto the Lord: "Verily, I have had three carpenters off ill. The gopher-wood supplier hath let me down—yea, even though the gopher wood hath been on order for nigh upon 12 months. What can I do, O Lord?"

And God said unto Noah: "I want that ark finished even after seven days and seven nights."

And Noah said: "It will be so."

And it was not so. And the Lord said unto Noah: "What seemeth to be the trouble this time?"

And Noah said unto the Lord: "Mine subcontractor hath gone bankrupt. The pitch which Thou commandest me to put on the outside and on the inside of the ark hath not arrived. The plumber hath gone on strike. Shem, my son who helpeth me on the ark side of the business, hath formed a pop group with his brothers Ham and Japheth. Lord, I am undone."

And the Lord grew angry and said: "And what about the animals, the male and the female of every sort that I ordered to come unto thee to keep their seed alive upon the face of the earth?"

And Noah said: "They have been delivered unto the wrong address but should arrive on Friday."

And the Lord said: "How about the unicorns, and the fowls of the air by sevens?"

And Noah wrung his hands and wept, saying: "Lord, unicorns are a discontinued line; thou canst not get them for love nor money. And fowls of the air are sold only in half-dozens. Lord, Lord, Thou knowest how it is."

And the Lord in His wisdom said: "Noah, my son, I knowest. Why else dost thou think I have caused a flood to descend upon the earth?"

One of the problems faced by Noah was how to get a job done on time. Here's a small example, and it raises the question: Do you want speed or quality?

390. A man was driven to desperation by the endless delays of the tailor who was making him a pair of pants. He said, "Tailor, in the name of heaven, it has already taken you six weeks!"

"So?" responded the tailor.

"So, you ask?" said the man. "Six weeks for a pair of pants? It took God only six days to create the universe."

"So," shrugged the tailor, "look at the shape it is in!"

Personnel Problems

391. Whom should we trust? That's a weighty question, so proven by the following story.

Baxter left his office for a few minutes. During his absence, Bassett stopped in. Later Bassett met Baxter in the hall:

Bassett: "You're a very careful fellow, Baxter."

Baxter: "What do you mean?"

Bassett: "Why, you locked all your drawers when you were only going to be gone for about five minutes. Do you really think it's likely that anybody would meddle with your things?"

Baxter: "Perhaps you are right, Bassett. But how did you find out that the drawers were locked?"

392. During a sales meeting, the manager was scolding all of the salespeople for the very poor sales of the company's products. He yelled, "All I hear is excuses! If you can't sell products that are truly great, maybe you should be replaced by people who can."

There was an awkward silence, and then a salesman, who was a retired professional football player, said, "Sir, this reminds me of my days in pro football. When the whole team was doing poorly, we usually got a new coach."

393. A manager of a large department got fed up with the occasionally irresponsible way people in the office were behaving. Knowing how compulsive his staff was about exercise and physical fitness, he prepared the following sign and posted it just inside the main office entrance:

NOTICE

This department requires
No physical fitness program.
Everyone gets enough exercise
Jumping to conclusions,
Flying off the handle,
Carrying things too far,
Dodging responsibilities,
And pushing his luck!

394. Despite his best efforts, the chief executive of a small company had trouble teaching an office boy proper professional decorum. Once the boy burst into his office, practically shouting, "Hey, can I have the afternoon off to see the ball game?" The executive sternly responded, "Wait a minute! You've got a few lessons to learn first, son. Trade places with me. You sit in my chair behind the desk, and I'll be you."

The young man sat behind the impressive desk, while his boss went out and tapped on the door.

"Come in," said the office boy.

"Excuse me, Sir," said the executive. "If you could spare me this afternoon, I would very much like to attend the ball game. Might I, Sir?"

"Sure thing," said the office boy, "and here's five dollars to help pay for your ticket."

Questionable Practices

395. Some years ago, a man found bedbugs in his hotel bed. As he checked out, he complained to the manager. A few days later, he received a very friendly letter explaining that, despite the best efforts of management and staff, such unfortunate incidents, although rare, did occasionally happen. The manager went on to thank him for calling the matter to his attention and expressed the hope that the man would accept his sincere apology.

He might have been inclined to do so, except that someone in the office had left a post-it slip on the letter that said, "Send this character the usual bedbug letter."

Business must make a profit, but the ways of doing this are not always entirely admirable.

396. Leslie Sauer, Adjunct Associate Professor of Landscape Architecture at the University of Pennsylvania, gave an address to a large gathering at the Annual Meeting of the Awbury Arboretum Association in Philadelphia. "One of our greatest problems," she said, "is that people tend to treat the earth like a business holding a liquidation sale."

She was roundly applauded.

397. General John Joseph Pershing (1860-1948) was one of America's most famous military men. He commanded army units in the Spanish-American War and the American Expeditionary Force (1917-1918) in World War I. Later in his life, he had to have teeth extracted. A few days after his visit to the dentist, the General heard that his teeth were being sold from souvenir stores in Washington for $7.50 a tooth. Pershing was very angry and sent some aides out to buy up all his molars and bicuspids. At the end of the day, the aides came back with 175 teeth.

Then it was Pershing teeth; today it's pieces of the Berlin Wall!

Clever Advertising

There's no question that ads and promotion can help increase sales and profit. Here are a few unusual examples.

398. Certainly death will come to all of us, so why not enjoy it in advance? Well, that seems to be the idea expressed in the following ad in *New England Monthly*.

LIFE COFFINS. Be reminded of the preciousness of your life every day. We sell a simple, honest, high-quality custom-sized rectangular pine box which comes ready for you to use as a bookcase or wine storage until you die.

399. Undertakers—now usually called funeral directors—often appear to anticipate the worst, or at least so it would seem if one takes seriously this ad in the *Tacoma Morning News Tribune*. It was promoting the services of the New Tacoma Funeral Home and Cemeteries, and said:

Our memorial counselors are skilled and sensitive professionals, and will gladly answer your questions or assist you with pre-need cremation or funeral arrangements.

(Not as bad, though, as the radio ad for the Woodlawn Cemetery that my wife and I heard while driving through California: "Is seepage disturbing your loved ones?")

400. Some shopkeepers can be subtly smart, and thereby make money. Take the case of the New York City florist Max Schling. He put an ad in the *Times* entirely in shorthand. Many businessmen, out of curiosity, asked their secretaries to translate it.

Translation: "When you want some beautiful flowers for your wife, remember Max Schling—low prices, top quality."

It worked; business boomed.

401. Just before his filling station, the proprietor had put up a large sign reading: "WE WILL FILL YOUR TANK FREE IF YOU CAN GUESS TO THE NEAREST HALF GALLON HOW MUCH IT TAKES."

A driver got into a line of cars, and when his turn came, he guessed wrong and so paid up. He asked the attendant, "How's your plan working?"

"Fine, fine," said the man. "A guy guessed right just about a year ago, and it cost me $8.35, but I don't have any more 'Gimme five gallons.' Everybody fills up."

402. Ah, the beautiful powers of well-selected bath ingredients! A delicious description of them is given in an advertisement for Kneipp Herbal Baths, made in West Hazelton, Pa. Under the heading "I BRING NATURE INTO MY BATH," it reads:

Comfort your mind and body with nature's herbal baths. Choose from ten herbal blends: ROSEMARY for waking up the system, HOPS—a calming bath at bedtime, MEADOW BLOSSOM—a pick-up bath after work, MELISSA gently soothing the senses, JUNIPER for unwinding after sport, SPRUCE and PINE to help lift the spirits, LAVENDER to combat fatigue, LINDEN and ORANGE BLOSSOM—becalming and relaxing, CAMOMILE—a gentle bath for the skin, EUCALYPTUS when the cold season comes.

403. In London there were two competing butcheries just across the street from each other. One butcher put up a sign in front of his shop reading: "We make sausage for Queen Elizabeth II."

A few days later his competition put up a sign in front of *his* shop. It read: "God Save the Queen!"

How to Succeed in Business—in Ingenious and Devious Ways

404. Henry Ford (1863-1947) was a practical man, and he greatly valued his time. It was his habit to drop into the offices of the plant executives he needed to talk with. One of these men asked him, "Mr. Ford, why don't you ask us to come to your office instead of coming to ours."

"Well, I'll tell you," said Ford. "I've found that I can leave the other fellow's office a lot quicker than I can get him to leave mine."

405. We all find ways to make ourselves feel important. "Self-esteem" is the modern term. A good case of it was displayed by the owner of a small railroad in Maine, which was called, if I remember correctly, the East Podunk, Burlap, and Western. The proud owner described it by saying, "It's only twelve miles long, but, by God, it's as wide as any goddam railroad in the country."

406. People in a jam often think up ingenious excuses. An example is the office boy who was asked by his boss when he came back to work: "Do you believe in life after death?"

"Oh, yes, I guess so," said the boy. "But why do you want to know?"

"Well, young man," said the boss, "I'm glad you do because after you had gone to your grandfather's funeral yesterday, he came here to talk to you."

407. Another ingenious kid, who will probably make a better businessman than arithmetician, came home from school one day and said, "Dad, if I saved you a dollar, would you give me fifty cents of it?"

Dad said, "That sounds reasonable, son. What's your proposition?"

"Remember, Dad, you said you'd give me a dollar if I passed arithmetic," said the boy. "Well, I saved you a dollar. I flunked it."

408. A certain underpaid teacher was a genius at pinching pennies. For instance, he never bought a new car —always a used (or "pre-owned") one. In this way, he saved lots of money, and the cars always seemed to run well with no major problems. A friend remarked, "I don't see how you do so well with the cars you buy. After all, you're a school teacher, not a mechanic."

"It's easy," replied the teacher. "I always insist on test-driving the car. Then I drive it to another used-car dealer and say I want to sell it to him. Right away, he examines the car and either tells me everything that's wrong with it or says he's ready to buy it. If he seems interested, I say, 'OK, I'll think about it,' and go back to the first dealer and make the purchase—at a considerably lower price."

409. A witty industrial executive, who also knew his Bible, agreed to teach a few sessions of Sunday School. He asked the children, "Why was Noah the first businessman?"

There was silence. Nobody knew.

"Well," said the executive, "it's because he floated the first joint stock company and forced all his competitors into involuntary liquidation."

410. A very practical man, discussing business and politics, uttered these words of wisdom: "Nothing is wrong with nepotism as long as you keep it in the family."

411. An equally practical businessman and father said impressively to his son, who was about to graduate from college: "The essentials for success in business are integrity and sincerity. If you can fake those, you'll rise to the top."

VP of Bovine Affairs

412. A big-city banker visited a farm to learn more about this important American activity. As the farmer was showing him around, he saw a man doing chores in the barnyard and asked, "Is that the hired man?"

"No," said the farmer, "that's the vice-president in charge of cows."

Three Pillars of Industry

413. Andrew Carnegie (1835-1919), a wise and practical man who made many millions of dollars in steel companies and gave over $350 million to charities, especially for peace and libraries, was once asked a trick question. "Mr. Carnegie, which is most important in industry—labor, capital, or brains?"

Carnegie replied, "Which is the most important leg of a three-legged stool?"

Risks, Profit-Sharing, and Motivation

414. George Eastman (1854-1932) was a creative inventor and industrialist, the creator of the Kodak camera (1888), and the founder of the Eastman Kodak Co. His gifts to philanthropy exceeded $100 million. He liked to travel, and once in Africa was manning a camera as a rhinoceros charged him. The rhino was only five feet away, but Eastman kept photographing the rhino until the man with him shot the beast dead.

Eastman's guide remonstrated, "What a risk!"

Eastman replied, "Well, you've got to trust your organization."

(Is this the secret of success in business?)

Of course businesses must make money, but, in the short run, even more important than over-all profit are employees' own wages or salaries.

415. An employer asked his sales manager suspiciously, "Do I detect the smell of liquor on your breath?"

"Yes, sir, you do," said the sales manager. "I've been celebrating the twentieth anniversary of the last raise you gave me."

416. The personnel manager of a large business kept a bowl of goldfish on his desk. Now and then he would stop work briefly, or even pause during an interview, and look fondly at the fish. A fellow worker asked him, "Sam, you seem to be very fond of those goldfish. Why?"

"Well," said Sam, "it's refreshing to have something in the office that opens its mouth and doesn't ask for a raise."

417. Business must be organized so that the workers, be they presidents, foremen, or common laborers, are motivated by a sense of purpose as they do their tasks. This is shown by an actual experience out in the field.

A labor force consisting of several men and a foreman had the job of digging holes and then filling them in right after digging them—seemingly for no reason. The digging was easy, the men were well paid, and the foreman was a nice guy. However, after the men had dug and filled in about sixty holes, they revolted. They felt the job was pointless, they had no sense of purpose, and so they said, in effect, "To hell with it!" They refused to dig any more.

Said one laborer, "Why the hell are we digging all these goddamned holes and then just filling them in? It's ridiculous."

"Oh, didn't I explain?" said the foreman. "We're trying to find an old water main that ran through this field."

That solved the labor problem. The *purpose* of the labor was made clear. From then on the men dug and filled the holes with good will, high energy, and satisfaction in their work.

The Universal Constant

This final story is not only relevant to business but to human relations in general.

418. The Northwest Mutual distributed this item to its staff, and eventually, I'm told by a friend who sent it to me, to many of its clients:

Mystery in the Office

I am an office mystery.
I am never seen, but I am everywhere.
I am always on the job and often forecast important events.
I make and unmake morals, reputations, and cooperation, but I am seldom blamed for my mistakes.
I have no responsibilities, and yet I am one of the most powerful molders of opinion.
I am quite as influential as other aspects of management, but I am never on an organization chart.
I am best known below administrative levels, and, though I criticize those in authority, no one can fire me.
I am rampant where administration is most severe, and yet I am active too when it is most kindly.
I am industrious wherever two get together, and I whisper with their laughter, disappointment, and fear.
I add humor and anger to the office as I pass with the speed of sound.
I am basic in human nature, and you must accept me.
I grow right behind you.
I am the office grapevine.

18

The Military

Wouldn't it be wonderful if the citizens of the earth could learn to live together without military forces? The day may come, but meanwhile do enjoy these few lighter tidbits about a heavy topic. The first six stories are presented in roughly chronological (historical) order.

Tales of the High and Mighty

419. One of General Ulysses S. Grant's (1822–1885) staff officers was well-known for his stupidity.
"Why do you keep Lieutenant Colonel Blank?" Grant was asked.
"Oh," said Grant, "he's very useful."
"Useful?" said the questioner. "How?"
"We could hardly get along without him," said Grant. "You see, when we issue an important and complicated order, we first give it to him to read. If he can understand it, we know that anybody can—and so we issue it."

420. Helmuth Graf von Moltke (1800–1891), the famous and successful Prussian field marshal who won the Austro-Prussian (1866) and Franco-Prussian wars (1870–1871), was famous for his ability to listen and to understand, and not to talk much. It was said of von Moltke, "He could keep his mouth shut in seven languages."

Maybe some of us could help make a better world by learning to do this in even one language!

421. Ypres (pronounced "eepr") is a small Belgian city where three terrible battles were fought during World War I. In October-November 1917, the British attacked the German line but were able to advance only five miles at a cost of 300,000 lives.

One of the surviving British Tommies, who had fought heroically and been severely wounded, was honored by a bedside visit from the wife of King George V, Queen Mary. The soldier told her all about the battle, pronouncing the place "Wipers." Each time he said "Wipers" the Queen quietlys aid "eepr." This happened several times.

After the visit a friend of the Tommy was asked how he enjoyed the visit. "Q " he said, "it was grand, and I was so impressed by 'ow friendly Her Majesty was." He paused. "The only strange thing was that she burped all the time."

422. One day in January of 1942, the captain of the battleship Washington, which was commanded by Admiral Forbes, heard a sailor yell, "Man overboard!"

The captain looked all around from the conning tower and ordered several other officers to do likewise. Nobody was sighted in the water. However, the sailor insisted, "But, sir, I saw someone fall over!"

So the captain mustered the entire crew of between 1,500 and 2,000 men, and *all* were present. As the captain was about to reprimand the sailor, someone murmured, "Has anyone seen the Admiral?"

423. In 1944, during World War II, I was a conscientious objector working abroad for the American Friends Service Committee. While in Cairo, I was suddenly called to go to Calcutta, India, to work with the Ramakrishna Mission distributing vitamins and powdered milk to Bengalis starving from a famine. I was amazed, when I applied for air passage, to be granted one at once. The army officer said, "Your work is very important.

I'm going to bump a colonel off the plane to make a space for you."

When I boarded the aircraft, an old C-47, I found myself—a C.O. civilian—surrounded by high-ranking officers. I suddenly had this thought: "I feel like a piece of china in a bullshop."

424. President Harry Truman (1884–1972) enjoyed an occasional trip on the Presidential yacht, the *USS Williamsburg*. It is said that on a frigid winter day in 1952, Truman came on deck to view the scene and get some fresh air. He saw a young sailor who was on deck watch. They engaged in some small talk, and then Truman said, "You look cold, son. Why don't you go down to the galley and get a cup of hot coffee?"

"Oh, Mr. President," replied the sailor, "I can't. I'm not allowed to leave my post."

Truman firmly took the sailor's rifle and said, "This is a command! Go down. Tell them the Commander-in-Chief sent you. I'll stand guard."

Winning at Any Cost

In military engagements, there's nothing more important than winning battles—even after the fact.

425. A Frenchman, after moving to England, gave up his French citizenship and became a British subject. One of his former countrymen asked, "Why? Why? What have you gained by it?"

"Well, for one thing," said the man, "I can now say we won the Battle of Waterloo."

426. A young officer was transferred to a new post. His colonel sent a letter to the new commanding officer, Colonel Maxfield, saying, among other things, "Lieutenant Wilcox is an able man, but he is a compulsive gambler. I suggest that you keep aware of this."

Colonel Maxfield summoned Wilcox. "Lieutenant, I understand that you are addicted to gambling. That's a bad habit. What sorts of things do you bet on?"

"Oh, anything, Sir," replied Wilcox. "For instance, I'll bet you $25 that you have a mole on your left shoulder."

"You bet that, do you?" said the Colonel sternly, and he took off his shirt and said, "See, no mole."

"Oh, well, I was wrong," said Wilcox and paid Colonel Maxfield.

Immediately, Maxfield telephoned the former colonel and told him what had happened. "I guess this will teach Wilcox a lesson," he said.

"I'm afraid not," said the former colonel. "Wilcox wins. Just before he left, he bet me $100 that he'd have your shirt off in ten minutes after he met you."

When we do lose "battles," perhaps it's best to lose them quickly.

427. A sergeant disobeyed orders and was commanded to go to the chief officer's tent. When he came out, he looked very downhearted. A friend asked, "What happened, Mike?"

"That officer sure is a man of few words," said the soldier.

"What do you mean?" asked his friend.

"He said to me, 'Sit down, sergeant; get up corporal; good-bye private.' "

The Voice of Authority

428. The new lieutenant of Company A was a small man but very strong. When he called the company to order for the first time, a bass voice from back in the ranks boomed, "And a little child shall lead them."

The next morning a notice was posted on the bulletin board. It read: "Company A will take a 25 mile hike today with full packs. And a little child shall lead them—on a damned big horse."

19

Smart Kid Answers—III

Yes, a little child shall, and did, lead them to success.

429. A large truck was making a delivery in a rural area. But as it went under a low bridge, the truck came to a grinding halt; the top of the van had got caught under the bridge. The driver tried to back up, but the truck wouldn't budge. A crowd of onlookers gathered, and everyone started giving all sorts of complicated advice about unbolting the bridge, removing the top section of the truck, etc., when a small boy casually remarked, "Why don't you just let some air out of the tires?"

The adults looked at the boy with dumbfounded expressions. It worked!

And here's a child who led his father—to nausea.

430. There was a very spoiled boy named Jeremy. His father decided to apply reverse psychology and let the kid have *anything* he wanted—to humor him completely.

Father: "All right, Jeremy, you can have anything you want for supper. Anything! So what do you want?"

Jeremy: "An earthworm."

So the father, grimacing, goes out, digs up a worm, and puts it on Jeremy's plate.

Father: "There you are, Jeremy. That OK?"

Jeremy (wailing): "I want the worm cooked!"

So the father fries the worm in a pan with butter and offers it again.

Jeremy (frowning): "You eat half the worm, Dad."

So the father does.

Jeremy (howling with anguish): "You ate my half!"

Some kids learn to be smart before they learn to be honest.

431. As the train's ticket collector proceeded down the aisle of a passenger car, he came to not-so-little Maureen. He said to her, "Children under twelve ride half-fare. How old are you?"

"Eleven," replied Maureen.

"Hmmm," mumbled the collector, "and when will you be twelve?"

"As soon as I get off the train," smiled Maureen.

Some kids appear to be smarter than their teachers, so perhaps there's hope for humankind.

432. It was arithmetic time in a small rural school. Mr. Fry, the teacher, asked the class, "If there were eleven sheep in a field and six jumped over the fence, how many would be left?"

Alison raised her hand and replied, "None."

"What do you mean, Alison?" said the teacher. "There would be five."

"There would not," said Alison. "Mr. Fry, you may know your arithmetic, but you don't know sheep."

433. There's more to arithmetic than arithmetic! A teacher asked, "If there were four flies on the table and I killed one, how many would be left?"

"One," answered a bright pupil, "the dead one."

434. Teachers should not be too quick to correct their pupils' responses. For example, when a third-grader named Frank was asked by his teacher to recite a sentence using the personal pronoun "I," he began, "I is . . ."

"No, Frank," the teacher interrupted. "Always say 'I am.'"

"Well, OK," said Frank. "I am the ninth letter of the alphabet."

435. Young pupils often come at problems from unexpected angles. Teachers should be careful not to squelch originality. For example, Miss Gilbert asked one of her third-grade students named Adam, "What is half of eight?"

"Which way?" asked Adam.

"What do you mean?" asked Miss Gilbert.

"I mean, on top or sidewise?" said Adam.

"Adam, I think that's a silly question," said the teacher.

"No, it's not, Miss Gilbert," said Adam. "The top half of eight is zero, but sidewise half of eight is three."

436. The spirit of enterprise begins young in some kids. A father gave his son a dollar for his birthday. For the next two hours, the boy went all over the neighborhood, getting his dollar changed into coins at one store, and the coins back into a dollar at the next. His father noticed and said, "Son, what's all this hustling around for?"

"Well, Dad, it's this way," replied the boy. "Sooner or later, somebody's going to make a mistake, and it's not going to be me."

437. I don't know how enthusiastic you are about museums, but my wife says that I get "museumitis" after 17 minutes in one of those places. A young girl I know is much more positive about visits to museums. Once her teacher took her class to visit the Natural History Museum in New York. That evening, her mother asked, "What happened at school today?"

"It was great!" replied the girl. "Our teacher took us to a dead circus."

Is history a dead circus? Read the next chapter and see.

20

History and Perspective

It is certainly helpful in understanding the world if we know a bit of history—and more than local history.

Some Significant Statistics

438. We all know the Bible story of Adam and Eve, but only in 1988 did geneticists discover, by tracing DNA trails, that "Eve" lived about 200,000 years ago, not the Biblical 5995 (as of 1991). Eve was dark-skinned and muscular and is your 10,000th great-grandma. She may have lived in Asia, but probably in sub-Saharan Africa. She was definitely not "Aryan" or WASP.

No scientist has found Adam yet!

439. Beings far larger than we humans lived eons ago. Here are some statistics about blue whales that may help you keep yourself in a properly modest perspective:

- They are the largest creatures who have ever lived.
- Compared to a brontosaurus, a major dinosaur, a blue whale would seem like a hippopotamus next to a hog.
- Blue whales weigh more than 2,500 human beings.

- Their tongues are ten feet thick and heavier than an elephant.
- Their hearts weigh half a ton and pump eight tons of blood.
- A blue whale's penis is ten feet long and weighs 100 pounds.

However, a blue whale could never figure out these things about human beings!

440. Certain statistics impress one and somehow seem to put the world, and even its proudest parts, into perspective. One of my favorites is that Lake Tahoe, which is between California and Nevada, is over 6,000 feet above sea level, has an area of 193 square miles, and in some places is 1,645 feet deep; there is enough liquid to cover all of California with 14 inches of water.

Local Perspectives

441. A Texan was showing a friend from Boston around the old chapel-fort known as the Alamo. He told the story of the great heroism of Davy Crockett (1786–1836) and the other 180 or so soldiers who were under siege by several thousand Mexican troops for eleven days in 1836. Even though they were defeated and all died, the cry, "Remember the Alamo!" rallied Texans to take up arms against the Mexicans and defeat them six weeks later. The Texan asked, "Did you ever hear of anyone so brave around Boston?"

"Did you ever hear of Paul Revere?" (1735–1818) asked the Bostonian.

"Oh, Paul Revere," said the Texan. "Isn't he the guy who ran for help?"

442. My wife and I spent a year in England and grew very fond of the people there—so polite, considerate, cordial, humorous, and friendly without ever imposing themselves upon you. One of the best things about Britain is the tea, not to mention the delicious accompaniments and pleasant conversation one usually finds at teatime. But the British can get in their sly digs at Americans. For instance, I remember hearing one American, at tea, exclaim, "Oh, I wish we could get such good tea at home," whereupon a pleasant lady at another table said, "But, my dear sir, we sent you a whole boatload and you threw it into the harbor!"

Another such dig—said with a twinkle—was made by some people we had just met. I quipped, "We come from Philadelphia. That's where we declared our independence from you!"

"Ah, yes," was the reply, "and I understand you've been going downhill ever since."

443. At a large dinner of a fraternal organization, guests were invited to rise and introduce themselves. One of the guests had immigrated from Russia a good many years ago, and he said: "I believe I am the only person who has become an American citizen with his clothes on."

444. When my wife and I were visiting the great Salisbury cathedral in England, we looked also in the Chapter House where is preserved for public view one of the four genuine copies of the Magna Carta (1215), a great document in the history of the struggle of liberty against oppression. As we were looking at the Magna Carta, a six-year-old American boy glanced at it and asked his parents, "Is that the thing George Washington wrote?"

He was gently corrected and then proceeded to look at another nearby area where a medieval frieze of sculptures representing scenes from the Old Testament was carved in stone. The boy, who was evidently Jewish, asked, "How come there's nothing about Jews here? It's not fair!" The British guide very tactfully informed him that all of the "cartoon" characters were Jews.

"Well, that's good," said the boy, with a big smile.

Wit Throughout the Ages

445. Charles Darwin (1809–1882), the great naturalist who established the theory of evolution, was visiting a friend in the English countryside. Two boys of the family thought they would play a trick on him, so they caught a grasshopper, a beetle, a centipede, and a butterfly. They carefully glued parts of each of these together and presented the strange creature to Darwin. "Mr. Darwin, sir," they asked, "can you identify this insect for us?"

Darwin looked at them, then at the creature, and asked, "Boys, did you notice whether it made a humming sound when you caught it?"

"Oh, yes, it did," they answered.

"Well, then," said Darwin, "it's a humbug."

446. In 1503, a rich young Italian girl wanted her portrait painted, and so she begged a famous artist she knew to paint her picture.

"I'm far too busy," said the artist. "But I'll tell you what. Why not ask that fellow da Vinci across the street, Mona? He needs the business."

447. Benjamin Franklin (1706–1790) was a wise man, but his wisdom did not always prevail. Because he knew a lot about nature, he felt that the turkey, not the eagle, should be the bird that symbolizes America. In 1784, he wrote:

I wish that the bald eagle had not been chosen as the representative of our country. He is a bird of bad moral character; he does not get his living honestly. You may have seen him perched on some dead tree where, too lazy to fish for himself, he watches the labor of the fishing hawk and, when that diligent bird has at length taken a fish and is bearing it to his nest for the support of his mate and young ones, the bald eagle pursues him and takes it from him . . . . besides, he is a rank coward; the little kingbird, not bigger than a sparrow, attacks him bodily and drives him out of the district. . . . For a truth, the turkey is in comparison a much more respectable bird.

448. Mark Twain (1835-1910) gave us perhaps the most challenging prescription for living. He said, "Let us endeavor to live so that when we come to die, even the undertaker will be sorry."

449. One of my favorite questions, since it compares two rather different figures, is: What did John the Baptist and Attila the Hun have in common?
The answer: Their middle names.

450. Senator Daniel Inouye (1924-   ) of Hawaii, who is of Japanese ancestry, gave a talk on "Our Kinship with the British People." When, during the question period, he was asked how he could possibly be the kin of Britons, he replied, "My great-great-great-great-grandfather ate Captain Cook."*

451. Mark Twain knew how to avoid wearying an audience. Once at a large banquet Twain was toasted as a great literary figure and asked to respond. He said, "Ladies and gentlemen, I am sorry to say that literature is in a pretty bad way. Shakespeare is dead and gone. Milton has been gathered to his fathers. Tennyson is no longer with us, and, ladies and gentlemen, I'm not feeling very well myself."
With that, he sat down.

452. Abraham Lincoln (1809-1865) is everybody's hero, at least north of the Mason-Dixon Line. When a fourth grader was required to write an essay on Lincoln, she began: "Abraham Lincoln was born on February 12, 1809, in a log cabin he built himself."
(By the way, log cabins aren't the great symbol of poor, rustic, hard-working folk they once were. Today, a well-made one goes for about $150,000.)

453. The humorist and philosopher Henny Youngman observed: "It's a funny thing. Abraham Lincoln once

---

*James Cook (1728-1779), the great English explorer, was killed by the natives on the Hawaiian Islands.

walked twenty miles to borrow a book. So now they close libraries to celebrate his birthday."*

Children on History

454. A fourth-grader, Kim, groaned as he was doing his history homework. His father noticed and asked, "What's the matter, Kim?"

Kim replied, "I *hate* history. It's so hard."

"Why, that's hard to understand," said the father. "I was always very good at history."

"Sure, Pop," said the boy, "it was easy for you. After all, you were there for most of it."

455. As a Quaker and a pacifist, I have disussed deeply and thoughtfully the problem of war. However, one day a seventh-grade girl, Letitia, gave me a reason for opposing armed conflict that I had never considered. She'd struggled with her homework; so when she came into class, she exclaimed for all to hear: "I hate wars. They cause too much history!"

456. A teacher was trying to bring out some of the less known yet interesting aspects of history. She asked, "What famous military men later went into other lines of work?"

A young girl eagerly raised her hand.

"Yes, Shirley?" said the teacher.

"General Eisenhower and Colonel Sanders," said Shirley.

Delusions of Grandeur

Perhaps people overestimate their own historical importance.

457. Where is the center of civilization, or where is its noblest expression? There are many answers to that

---

*from Henny Youngman's *All-Time Greatest One-Liners* (Pinnacle).

question, none of them correct. However, there are some places where there is a blind (confident?) certainty as to the answer. This is illustrated by something that happened at Cambridge University, England, founded in the early twelfth century. Just after the outbreak of World War I in 1914, a young woman accosted a don (a weighty professor) and demanded, "What are you doing to defend Civilization?"

"Madame," replied the don, "I *am* the Civilization that is being defended."

458. A young, able, aspiring actor was attempting to persuade his landlord to wait a few weeks for the rent. "Just think," he said, "in a few years tourists will pass by this apartment and say, 'Look! That's the apartment where the famous actor Kirk Simons once lived.' "

The landlord replied, "If you don't pay the rent today, they'll be able to say that tomorrow."

Moving with the Flow

We're all a part of history and in probably minor ways (keep that perspective!) can affect it and help move civilization forward.

459. Jane Rushmore, who was an elderly Quaker when I was a mere boy, was concerned that Quakers were becoming too conservative—looking backward rather than forward. One Sunday, she rose in Meeting for Worship and said concisely, "Friends, the landmarks set by our forefathers were meant to be landmarks, not campsites."

So, Friends (Quakers) and friends, don't just camp out; move forward.

460. George Bernard Shaw (1856-1950) enjoyed more than anyone else I know pricking egotistical balloons and undermining clichés. Example: "The reasonable person adapts himself to the world; the unreasonable one persists in trying to adapt the world to himself. Therefore, all progress depends upon the unreasonable man."

21

Old Age

When most people (except for us oldsters—I'm 73 as I write these words) think of "old age," they think of people in that age group as being, on the whole, pretty miserable. Well, it ain't so! Careful studies prove it. When it comes to sad problems like loneliness, bad health, poor medical care, not enough to do, inadequate housing, or not enough friends, 45 percent of U.S. citizens think all of these problems are true of oldsters. *But:* only 5 percent of the "aged" think so. They are enjoying life!*

Secrets of a long Life

So how do you enjoy life? By avoiding unnecessary clutter and housekeeping.

> **461.** A widow lived to be well into her nineties. On her birthdays, she always gave a little party for her friends and relatives, and they routinely brought her a small gift, such as a knick-knack for her apartment. One year, a friend phoned and asked, "What would you like for your birthday this year?"
> "Oh, just give me a kiss," said the old woman. "Then I won't have to dust it."

---

*For more details, and a lot of other facts and individual, witty utterances about old age, get my book *Older and Wiser—Wit, Wisdom, and Spirited Advice from the Older Generation* (New York: Walker Publishing Company, 1986).

And how do you keep from being bored on a long trip? It's not so easy for the young, but for oldsters there's a good solution.

462. An elderly gentleman on a train was mumbling to himself, smiling, and then raising his hand. After a moment of silence, he would go through the same process: mumble, smile, raise hand, silence.

Another passenger observed this, and after about an hour, he said, "Pardon me, sir. Is anything wrong?"

"Oh, no," replied the oldster. "It's just that long trips get boring so I tell myself jokes."

"But why, sir," asked the passenger, "do you keep raising your hand?"

"Well," said the oldster, "that's to interrupt myself because I've heard that one before."

463. It's important to get things into perspective, and older people are usually better able to do this than younger ones. A prime example is George Burns (1896–). A reporter asked him, "Is it true that you smoke fifteen to twenty cigars a day, drink four or five martinis, and chase girls?"

"Yes, it is," replied Burns.

"Well, goodness," said the reporter. "What does your doctor say?"

Burns replied, "My doctor's dead."

Experience Pays

464. An old-timer named Jake, who lived in a medium-sized town, had worked for years on the public electric system. After he had been retired for a couple of years, there was a violent thunderstorm, and the lightning knocked out the town's electricity. Experts were called in and tried everything they could to restore the current, but nothing worked. After two days without electricity, someone said, "Let's ask Jake. He always got things fixed."

So they did, saying, "Don't worry. Even though you're retired we'll pay you if you can do the job."

So Jake took a long ladder, walked to a certain pole, set up the ladder, climbed it, and tapped a certain wire. Immediately the lights went on all over town! The next day, Jake presented his bill. It was for $1,000.

"What!?" exclaimed the town treasurer. "Why it didn't take you longer than ten minutes to do the job. How do you justify such a large bill?"

So Jake itemized it:

Climbing a ladder and tapping a wire.... $5.00
Knowing where to tap................. $995.00
　Total........................ $1,000.00

Jake was paid.

465. An old football coach, who had always been very energetic and successful, finally retired. When someone asked him, "Coach, how do you like it?" he replied, "It's great! Now I don't do anything—and I don't start till noon."

Aging Gracefully with Tongue in Cheek

They say that old people go into a decline. Well, in some ways it's true, but in other ways it's a benign decline, taken with good humor.

466. Toward the end of her life, Sarah Bernhardt (1844-1923), who was considered the queen of French romantic tragedy, lived in an apartment high above the streets of Paris. One evening she received a visit from an old admirer who climbed the many stairs to reach her apartment. When she opened her door, she found him panting from the long climb.

"Madame Bernhardt," exclaimed the admirer, "why do you live so high up?"

"Oh, mon cher ami," Bernhardt replied, "it's the only way I can still make the hearts of men beat faster."

467. A friend of mine at Germantown Friends School, now age 68, wrote me the following description of her athletic activities:

Our Senior Doubles Tennis group looks rather like a bunch of separating amoebas with every joint tied up with Ace bandages. One cynical fellow in the group recently referred to us as "The Forest Lawn Tennis Association," but I told him: "The only difference between us and the pros is that they grunt when they serve and we grunt when we lean over to pick up the balls!"

Ah well, *Tempus* does *fugit*.

468. In nursing homes—better called life-care communities—sometimes the residents tend to forget recent details of life, or even major events. Evidence: one old lady met another coming down the corridor and asked, "Was it you or your sister who died yesterday?"

469. This bit of dialogue actually occurred in a life-care community where a friend of mine resides. One woman greeted another as they were going to breakfast, saying, "Good morning. My name is Franny Rhoads. Do you remember what your name is?"

470. An old man finally purchased an inconspicuous in-the-ear hearing aid. He was told he could return it if he wasn't satisfied. Ten days later, he came back to the audiologist's office. "I just want to tell you how pleased I am," he said.

"Your family probably likes it too," commented the doctor.

"Oh, goodness, they don't even know I've got it," chuckled the old man. "But I'm having a wonderful time with it. In just two weeks I've changed my will twice."

The Terminology of Old Age

You may have noticed that in this chapter, frankly titled "Old Age," I've occasionally used the term "oldster." One can also say "old person" or "older person," but *not* "crone" (female) or "geezer" (male). However, when one of our daughters drops by for a visit, she sometimes says, with a big smile, "Just making a geezerosity check."

What about the term *aging*?

471. Mal Schechter is on the faculty of the Ritter Department of Geriatrics and Adult Development at the Mt. Sinai School of Medicine, New York. He strongly objects to the word "aging." Whereas wine and whiskey are supposedly better after they have aged, what about people? Schechter makes the following points:

- Aging baseball players are in their 30s.
- From the day they are born, people are aging.
- Sun-blocking agents are called "anti-aging." Says Schechter: "Smear on too much and you surely return to childhood."

We talk about an "aging airliner," with "metal fatigue." Why not a "fatigued" airliner? (And what live pilot is not aging?)

So, suggests Schechter, why not have: "U.S. Senate Special Committee on Delapidation"; "the White House Conference on Crumbling"; "the Federal Council on Wreckage"; and "the U.S. Administration on Decay"?

So, concludes Schechter: "Let's retire 'aging.' From infant to great-grandparent, all of us are getting older."

Also, say I, we don't die of old age; we die because of a disease. Old age is a great time of life!

Die Laughing

But eventually we all die, and I'm a strong believer in the right to die—a good death, not a prolonged, painful, and expensive one. However:

472. Zachariah, a well-known figure in a small town, was given a birthday party by fellow citizens to celebrate his eighty-fifth birthday. At the party, a friend asked, "Now admit it, Zack: don't you hate to grow old?"

"Hell, no," Zachariah answered. "If I wasn't old, I'd be dead."

473. A dying Scotsman summoned his best and oldest friend, Bill, to his bedside.

"Bill," he said, "I'm goin' fast, and a favor I want to ask of ye. This bottle of whiskey is the finest of the fine—now 103 years old, and I won't be able to drink it, so I want you to do something for me. After they get me into the ground, I want you to take the bottle out to the cemetery and pour it all on my grave. Will ye do it, Bill?"

"Of course I'll do it," Bill replied, "but do ye mind if, when I come to pour it on your grave, I run it just one time through me kidneys?"

474. Two youngsters were talking about their families, and one asked, "Why does your grandmother spend so much time reading the Bible?"

"I don't know," replied the other, "but I think she's cramming for her finals." (Which reminds me of another lady who, very late in life, took up the study of Hebrew. When asked why, she replied, "I want to be able to speak to God in His own language.")

The Twilight Years

We'll close this chapter with a classic account of a youngster's visit to his grandparents in a life-care community.

475. After Christmas vacation, a teacher asked her small pupils to write an account of how they spent their holidays. One boy wrote as follows:

We always spend Christmas with Grandma and Grandpa. They used to live up here in a big red house, but Grandpa got retarded and they moved to Florida.

They live in a place with a lot of retarded people. They live in tin huts. They ride big three wheel tricycles. They go to a big building they call a wrecked hall but it is fixed now. They play games there and do exercises, but they don't do them very good. There is a swimming pool and they go to it and just stand there in the water with their hats on. I guess they don't know how to swim.

My Grandma used to bake cookies and stuff. But I guess she forgot how. Nobody cooks—they all go out to fast food restaurants.

As you come into the park, there is a doll house with a man sitting in it. He watches all day, so they can't get out without him seeing them. They wear badges with their names on them. I guess they don't know who they are.

My Grandpa and Grandma worked hard all their lives and earned their retardment. I wish they would move back home but I guess the man in the doll house won't let them out.

22

Manners, Good and Bad

Webster's Ninth New Collegiate Dictionary defines *manners* thus: "habitual conduct or deportment: BEHAVIOR (mind your —s)." We'll begin this chapter with three stories which illustrate bad—though possibly justified—manners.

Bad Manners Sometimes Fit the Occasion

476. Baseball umpires have a tough life, with so many close calls to make. They are often challenged for not doing their job right. A good illustration of their problems came one afternoon when, as a trio of umpires walked onto the field, the band loudly played "Three Blind Mice."

477. Bloomingdale's was having a big sale with an especially good price on nylons. A well-mannered gentleman decided to buy his wife a pair. He got caught in a crowd in front of the counter and suddenly found himself being banged, buffeted, and hit by frantic women bargain-hunters. Finally, realizing that he was being forced back rather than going forward, he decided to take action. Lowering his head, he flailed his arms and plowed through the crowd. "Hey, you!" shouted a shrill voice. "Can't you act like a gentleman?"

"Hell," he roared, "I've been acting like a gentleman for half an hour. Now I'm acting like a lady."

478. At a traditional wake, friends of the deceased were first invited to the viewing, and then the ladies sat in the parlor, knitting and sipping tea, while the gentlemen enjoyed themselves in another room with somewhat stronger beverages.

One of the gents who had imbibed a bit too much staggered out of the room muttering, "I think I'll go and view our friend again." In his state of mind he quickly lost his way and went into a room with a large upright piano. Approaching the piano solemnly, he knelt before it, glanced down at the keys, and exclaimed admiringly, "My, didn't he have a grand set of teeth!"

Keeping a Civil Tongue

479. The *Western Morning News* described the following play-stopping incident which took place during a big cricket match between England and Australia in West Cornwall, England, in 1989. The manner in which the event is described is a good example of British reserve and delicacy:

Brunette Sheila Nichols stopped play . . . by streaking starkers across the hallowed cricket ground. The shapely nineteen-year-old University of Essex student stripped naked at the Nursery End and then bounced the length of the field to the cheers of twenty-five thousand spectators.

With the English and Australian players watching intently, she left a puffing steward in her wake and then topped the performance with a perfect cartwheel right in front of the Cricket Club members.

And here's the climax, an example of typical English understatement: "Police said she would be cautioned for possible breach of the peace."

480. Extreme politeness on the part of a witness caused this tongue-in-cheek circumlocution in court one day:

Lawyer: "Mr. Osgood, do you mean to say that Mrs. Klauder, our previous witness, is a liar?"

Mr. Osgood: "Oh, no, I merely wish to make it clear what a liar I am if Mrs. Klauder is speaking the truth."

Professional Manners, Mannerisms, and Courtesy

If you are a professional, especially one who feels superior to others, manners have their place.

481. Waiters, especially in elegant English restaurants, often feel superior to their customers but are not allowed to argue. One such waiter said to an uncouth customer, "Sir, my position does not permit me to answer you back. But if it ever came to a choice of weapons, Sir, I should choose grammar."

482. Thaddeus Stevens (1792–1868), a famous American abolitionist, statesman, and lawyer, had just finished arguing a case before the court and did not like the ruling of the judge. "Old Thad" turned scarlet and his lips quivered. With trembling hands, he began to pack up his papers, ready to quit the courtroom. The judge observed all this and said angrily, "Do I understand, Mr. Stevens, that you wish to show your contempt for this court?"

"No, Your Honor," Stevens replied. "I'm trying my best to conceal it."

483. A minister, a lawyer, and a doctor were boating along the shoreline of shark-infested waters when their outboard motor conked out. The wind and waves buffeted their boat so violently back and forth that a set of oars fell out and drifted away in the current. "One of us will have to swim ashore and go for help," said the doctor.

"I'll do it," said the lawyer and at once dove into the sea and struck out for shore. As the doctor and minister watched, the lawyer swam right between the fins of the sharks and reached the beach safely.

"My God," said the minister, "we've seen a miracle!"

"Oh, no," replied the doctor. "It was just a matter of professional courtesy."

The Rules of Polite Society

484. Nebraska appears to be undergoing a process of degentrification, to judge by the following report from *The Omaha World Herald* in 1989:

> Muffy Fisher Vrana, etiquette consultant for Marjabelle Young-Stewart's "White Gloves and Party Manners" and "Poise for Preteens" programs in Lincoln, has announced a name change in classes for girls ages 5 to 12.
>
> "The negative connotations of 'white gloves' and 'poise' have met with some resistance from mothers of young girls," Mrs. Vrana said.
>
> Thus, the classes have been renamed "Winning Attitudes" for 5-to-8-year-olds and "Power Pack for Preteens" for girls ages 9–12.

How are the etiquette consultants doing in your town?

485. A friend gave me a worn copy of a book titled *The Young Man's Handbook of Etiquette,* published in Philadelphia by an unnamed author, perhaps a hundred years ago. The Preface is worth reading today:

> The object of this work is to instruct those who have not been familiar with the world, in the customs and usages of good society; and to explain those principles of good-breeding which every man should be
>
> "Wax to receive and marble to retain."
>
> Of the regulations of etiquette, we willingly say, "Nos haec novimus esse nihil;" they are trifles; they are nothing. But in human life, trifles are often of immense importance; and little as these precepts may seem, an acquaintance with them is perfectly indispensable.

So, dear reader, be wax to receive and marble to retain the principles of politeness. If you do, civilization will be advanced!

486. George Bernard Shaw (1856–1950) had little time for the high social classes, nor for those who sought his company because he was a celebrity. Shaw received this invitation: "Lady Grosvenor will be at home on Thursday between four and six."

He returned the card with this note written at the bottom: "Mr. Bernard Shaw likewise."

Sassy Kids with Occasional Manners

487. Children can sometimes be very polite but also disconcertingly honest. For example, a lady said to a small girl, "How do you do, my dear?"

"Fine, thank you," replied the girl.

There was a pause and then the lady said, "Why don't you ask me how *I* am?"

"Because," replied the girl pleasantly, "I'm not interested."

488. Six-year-old Pauline was beautifully behaved, obedient, helpful, and polite all during a party her parents were giving at their house. But as soon as the last guest left, Pauline turned snarly and disobedient.

Her mother asked, "Dearie, why are you so naughty now? It was wonderful what a little lady you were all during the party."

"Well, Mom," Pauline answered, "you don't use your company silver all the time, do you?"

Faux Pas

489. A rather proper man was seated next to his hostess at a dinner party. He was very embarrassed because the dinner was rather gassy and he couldn't restrain himself from passing wind.

The hostess glanced at the floor and said, "Go away, Fido."

The man was relieved, but again he had the urge, and again, with somewhat less hesitation, he let go.

The hostess, glancing at her guest and then at the dog, repeated, "Fido, go away!"

It came upon him a third time and this time he simply, without hesitation, farted once more.

Finally, the hostess loudly exclaimed, "Go away, Fido. I said *go*—before he shits on you."

All Creatures Great and Small

England is a country where good manners are displayed even toward worms.

490. In May 1989, my wife and I stayed at the South Sands Hotel, near Dartmouth, West Devon, England. We saw a sign announcing "The Worm Charming Championships" to take place on Monday, a "Bank Holiday." Here are the rules and practices:

Each team shall have three players: (1) a charmer; (2) a catcher; (3) a counter.

Object: to coax as many worms as possible out of your allotted patch of ground in the given time.

Permitted stimulants: watering (traditional); Heavy Metal Music.

After the championship is awarded, all worms must be returned to their respective holes.

23

Signs of Life—IV

491. More signs I have observed over the years, some funny, some deadly serious:

- In a kitchen: If the icebox catches on fire, ring the towel.

- In a restaurant: Don't tip the waiters—it upsets them.

- Another eatery: Eat here—why go somewhere else to be cheated?

- Yet another food joint: Come in and eat before we both starve.

- At a store: In God we trust; all others pay cash.

- Another store: Credit extended to those over 80 if accompanied by their grandparents.

- Yet another store: Your face is good, but it won't go in the cash register.

- And a couple of beer joints: (1) We don't sell any beer on Sundays and mighty darn little during the week.
  (2) Our beer contains vitamin P.

- Above the door of a physical therapy room in a nursing home in Olathe, Kansas: "Faith, Hope, and Therapy."

- In a science lab: Tragedy is the murder of a beautiful theory by a brutal gang of facts.

- In a science lab: The fewer the facts, the stronger the opinion.

- On a marriage counselor's door: Back in an hour. Don't fight.

- On a ski slope: Going beyond this point may result in death and/or loss of skiing privileges.

492. Signs from various institutions and public buildings:

- On the National Archives Building in Washington: What is past is prologue. (A taxi driver explained to a tourist that the words meant, "Brother, you ain't seen nothin' yet.")

- On a church bulletin board: Atheists are people with no invisible means of support.

- Inscribed on a prison: Cease to do evil. Learn to do well. (George Bernard Shaw, who reported this sign, remarked that it was on the outside where the prisoners couldn't read it.)

- At the entrance to a school administration building: Education will broaden a narrow mind, but there is no known cure for a big head.

- On an English warehouse: No smoking in case of fire.

- In a cemetery: No trespassing. Violators will be haunted.

- On the entrance of the Gate of Heaven Cemetery: Gates close at 4:30.

- At the bottom of a church bulletin board: A cheerful heart is a good medicine. . . . But a downcast spirit dries up the bones.
—Proverbs 17:22

493. Now three signs in England which, each in its own way, say something about the English way of life.

- At the bar of the Gara Rock Hotel, England, posted below a trumpet with a rubber squeeze bulb: If needing urgent lubrication, trumpet and squeeze.

- In the bathroom (W.C.s) of the Riverside Hotel in Helford, England:
    > Please put nothing obstructive down the loo.
    > Our drains block easily.

- In Harrod's department store in London: Please try not to smoke.

24

Art and Artists

There are many forms of art: theater, painting, sculpture, dancing, music, writing. We'll start with music.

Putting a Prodigy in His Place

494. Mischa Elman (1891–1967) was a world-renowned violinist, born in Russia. He first gained prominence in Berlin at age thirteen, but he had been playing long before that. He recalled, "I was an urchin of seven, and I flattered myself that I rattled off Beethoven's 'Kreutzer Sonata' finely. The sonata has in it several long, impressive rests. During one of these rests, a motherly old lady leaned forward, patted my shoulder, and said, 'Play something you know, Dear.' "

Keeping Them on Their Toes

495. I happen not to be a ballet enthusiast, and therefore I greatly sympathize with a young boy who was taken by his mother to *The Nutcracker Suite*. As he watched the women dancers skitter about on their toes, he looked puzzled. He asked, "Mom, why don't they just get taller ladies?"

A Picture Worth a Thousand Words

496. Sometimes art is the best way to illustrate simple truths or misunderstandings. An example is the Sunday School class which was told the story of Adam and Eve and was then asked to draw a picture illustrating any part of the story. Lilly drew a car with three people in it, a man in the front seat, and a man and a woman in the back seat.

"Lilly," asked the teacher, "will you please explain your picture?"

"Why," replied Lilly, "it's obvious. This is God driving Adam and Eve out of the garden."

A Real Bomb

497. A bad play had a short run on Broadway. After the first performance two critics were discussing the matter.

Critic 1: "I'm amazed that the audience didn't hiss."

Critic 2: "Well, it's very hard to hiss and yawn at the same time."

Architecture: Natural Form Vs. Pretentious Artifice

498. Architects often struggle to develop a good concept for a project, and then they keep struggling to make it all turn out right. Sometimes it is best not to try to plan everything in advance. Christopher Williams, in his excellent *Origins of Form*, demonstrates this aspect of architecture. He writes:

A leading architect once built a cluster of office buildings set in a central green. The landscape crew asked him where he wanted the sidewalks between the buildings. His reply: "Just plant grass between the buildings." By late summer the new lawn was laced with pathways of trodden grass. The paths followed the most efficient line between the points of connection, turned in easy curves rather than at right angles and were sized according to traffic flow. In the fall the architect simply paved in the pathways. Not only did the paths have a design beauty, but they responded directly to user needs.

499. Bathrooms are a part of the nitty-gritty of architecture. But the right advertising can make them seem like the seat of luxury and extravagance in a home. For instance, have you considered a really artistic set of bathroom spigots? Do you admire Renaissance art? Do you enjoy extravagant claims? If you answer yes to any of these, you will appreciate this ad in the California paper *The Laguna Beach Coast Line*:

Raphael [1483-1520], the Master Artist of the Renaissance Period. Known for his sense of color, form and passion, he became a legend in his own time. And now, comes Raphael Faucets, the rebirth of design and finer quality in solid brass faucets, tubsets and accessories.

Posing Nude

500. There's no doubt that the British have a sensible way of looking at things. A recent phenomenon in England is "streaking"—running across a public place totally nude. In a letter to the *Daily Telegraph*, 8 June, 1989, Gilham Moore, an artist's model from Middlesex, wrote:

SIR—I am interested in Nicholas Usherwood's letter about nakedness, nudity and embarrassment following the Lord's streak. As an experienced nude model for art classes, I have never seen any sign of embarrassment among members of a class even when some of them are attending a life class for the first time.

For instance, when I have failed to get back into exactly the same pose after a break, members of the class, be they male or female, pensioners or teenage A-level students, have never shown any embarrassment whatever in talking to me and telling me so despite the fact that I am sitting or standing in front of them without any clothes on.

I think that embarrassment at a display of nudity depends on it occurring at an inappropriate time and place.

Reverence for Art

501. On West 43rd Street in New York City, there is a fake tombstone created by the sculptor Alex Nixon. Beside it graze four plastic flamingoes. On the stone is inscribed: "DIVINE: Rest in Polyster." Near this unusual memorial the artist has set up a miniature Noah's ark.

Nixon says that he has seen people pass the monument and cross themselves!

Modern Arts: Cacophony and Chaos

502. These days, you never know what a "modern" band is going to sound like. For example, someone asked a member of a moderately exclusive club, "How's the orchestra?"

"Well, who am I to say it's bad," replied the club member.

"You don't sound very enthusiastic," commented the inquirer.

"You're right," said the member. "Last night when a waiter dropped a tray of dishes, five couples got up to dance."

503. Three teenagers were touring a modern art gallery. They realized they were alone in a room full of broken glass, twisted pipes, splintered wood, and grossly tangled shapes.

"Gad!" said one of them. "Let's get out of here before they accuse us of wrecking the place!"

Life Imitating Art

504. Raoul Dufy (1877-1953), the famous French illustrator, decorator, and painter, was very talented at glorifying his subjects, whether they were landscapes, seascapes, or people. He was also a master at promoting his own work. Example: When Dufy had finished a portrait of a rich and important client, the subject said, "But it doesn't look like me."

"Well, why not try looking like your portrait?" replied Dufy.

25

Writing and Writers: Good and Bad, All Generations

I'm a writer. In fact, in 1977 I gave up teaching junior high school in order to spend nearly full time on writing. It may not be a nobler task, but it lets you control your own hours (except for publishers' deadlines) and it earns you more money. Not counting this book, I have authored or co-authored 52 books, and they've sold over 21 million copies. Some of my books, though, have been "remaindered" (sold cheap, no royalties) and some have suffered the ultimate humiliation: they have been shredded to make room in the warehouses for more successful volumes.

Despite all this, I cannot claim to be a famous writer. But even famous writers get their share of criticism.

Critical Disdain

> **505.** Even the greatest literary giants must be seen in perspective, especially in England. I read an example of this in the Royal Shakespeare Company's program notes for *Hamlet*. It said that "Shakespeare was not highly esteemed critically as a playwright. With the exception of Ben Johnson (1572-1637), his contemporaries looked down on him as a hackwriter who was not, like most other dramatists of the period, a university man. Robert Greene (1558?-1592), 'a university wit,' called him 'an upstart crow.' "

506. Robert Benchley (1889-1945), drama critic for *Life* and *The New Yorker*, as well as author of *My Ten Years in a Quandry* (1936), confessed to a friend that it took him fifteen years to discover that he had no talent for writing. "But," he continued, "by then it was too late. I couldn't give up writing because I was too famous."

Presidential Prose and Poetry

507. Presidents of the United States have many heavy duties, but it is surprising that some of them before or after being President, have written rather unusual books. Here are six:

Poems of Religion and Society, by John Quincy Adams (1768-1848; President, 1825-1829)

Legacy of Fun, by Abraham Lincoln (1809-1865; President, 1861-1865)

Hunting Trip of a Ranchman, by Theodore Roosevelt (1858-1919; President, 1901-1909)

On Being Human, by Woodrow Wilson (1856-1924; President, 1913-1921)

Principles of Mining, by Herbert Hoover (1874-1964; President, 1929-1933)

Where's the Rest of Me?, by Ronald Reagan (1911- ; President, 1981-1989)

Small Gems

508. It's probably good from time to time to get outside your own body and consider its uses objectively. The English essayist, poet, and statesman Joseph Addison (1672-1719), a master of precise and orderly prose and publisher of a daily periodical called *The Spectator*, wrote on July 12, 1711: "I consider the Body as a System of Tubes and Glands, or to use a more Rustick phrase, a Bundle of Pipes and Strainers, fitted to one another after so wonderful a manner as to make a proper Engine for the Soul to work with."

509. An English professor asked his students to write a story involving these four subjects: religion, health, sex, and mystery. One student wrote, "Oh, my God, I'm pregnant! I wonder who?"

510. Jean Kerr (1923-   ), a journalist and writer and the author of *Please Don't Eat the Daisies* (1957), is a genius at many things, especially in the puncturing of clichés. (There's a mixed metaphor!) On the subject of beauty she wrote: "I'm tired of all this nonsense about beauty being only skin-deep. That's deep enough. What do you want, an adorable pancreas?"

511. Brevity in writing is often a virtue, and it's especially important for newspaper editors to shorten their reporters' submissions. The people who do this for editors are called rewrite men.

A few years ago, an editor needed a new rewrite man. When a young fellow applied, the editor said, "OK, here's a test of your skill. Fix this text, and especially shorten it, but don't lose any of the essential ideas and subleties."

With that, he handed the applicant a copy of the Ten Commandments. The young man read it through carefully and then went over to a desk and quickly and definitely made changes. "Here," he said, "this ought to do it."

The new rewrite man had written "Don't" ten times.

Howlers

512. Sometimes newspapers make big, hilarious mistakes, and then, when they try to correct them, the result is even funnier. Here's an example from Alabama:

In some editions of *The Birmingham News* Tuesday, paragraphs from a study of American sexual behavior were mistakenly included in a story on the Dead Sea Scrolls. The two stories are unrelated.

513. Bret Harte (1836-1902) edited a small newspaper in California, *The Overland Monthly*. (Later, he wrote the famous *The Luck of Roaring Camp* and *The Outcasts of Poker Flat,* and he even became U.S. Counsul in Germany and Scotland [1878-85].) When the wife of a leading citizen died, he wrote a eulogy about her, concluding, "She was distinguished for charity above all the other ladies of this town."

After writing the piece, Harte stopped by the office to look at the proofs. He reported:

I found that the intelligent compositor had made me say, "She was distinguished for chastity above all the other ladies of this town." I crossed out the insulting s, put a big query mark in the margin and went home. To my horror in the morning I read, "She was distinguished for chastity(?) above all the other ladies of this town."

514. Jeremy graduated from a school of journalism and got a job as a reporter on a small paper. The editor instructed him: "Never write anything as a fact unless you are absolutely certain about it. That way, you'll keep the paper out of trouble. Use words like, 'it was said,' 'alleged,' 'reputed,' 'claimed,' or 'rumored.' "

Jeremy was very conscientious. Here is his first report:

It is rumored that a party was given yesterday by a number of reputed ladies. Mrs. Gable, it was said, was hostess, and the guests, it is alleged, with the exception of Mrs. Curtis, who says she is fresh from Seattle, were all local people. Mrs. Gable claims to be the wife of Alfred Gable, rumored to be the president of an alleged bank.

Bad Writing Is Hard Work

515. Sometimes a dramatic trick can increase students' motivation to do well—perhaps even more than high and low marks.

For example, a professor of English at a top university I shall not name read to his class a very poorly written essay. "All right," he said, "have you any comments?"

The class tore the essay apart in general and in detail. Then the professor said, "Hmm. Well, it so happens I wrote that paper myself."

An embarrassed silence came over the class, but the teacher went on: "You're right. It is a terrible piece of work, and it took me two hours last night to compose it. I wanted to be sure I had not omitted a single feature of bad writing." He paused, and then said, "What amazes me is how you students can dash these things off day after day in ten minutes."

Unauthorized

Are there any advantages to being a well-established writer? Well, here's a story about one writer who tried to get an advantage.

516. A man, driving a rather oldish-looking car, and looking very self-confident and thoughtful with his pipe in his mouth, was proceeding along the expressway, when he came to one of those openings between the lanes. Despite a bold "NO U TURN" sign with the warning "Authorized Vehicles Only," he turned into the opening and stopped, got out a book and a pencil, and started working. Soon, a patrol car with its lights flashing drove in beside the man.

"Say, Buddy," shouted the cop, "can't you read? It says 'Authorized vehicles only'!"

"Of course, I can read," said the man, "and write, too. I just had to pull over and jot down this idea before I forgot it. I'm an author, I've owned this car for ten years, and hence it's completely *authorized*."

The author didn't tell me what action the trooper took, but he's still writing, and I have a feeling he probably won the war of words.

However, I've never dared to try the same thing.

Write with the Honesty of Children

Some of the most delightful writing is done by kids. Sometimes the delights are unintentional.

517. As I was jogging near a local middle school, I picked up a rumpled note that an eighth grader had dropped. It was written, according to the heading, for "V. Comm." class—Visual Communication. Here are the rules for V. Comm., or some of them:

There will be no excuse for arriving late to class. . . . Unexcused lateness will result in a lowered behavior grade.

Quickly and quietly enter the room and go directly to your assigned seat.

Be courteous (an expression of respect).

Gum chewing and other foods are not permitted. . . .

If you need a bathroom pass, you must make the tall pass and the teacher will sign it. . . .

Each student is expected to perform to his/her full potential. . . .

You are here to learn, create, use your imagination, and have fun.

518. Vivid prose is sometimes written by young children. Often, perhaps, they do not fully realize all the implications of what they write. The following, which I picked up from the gutter of our street, was composed by a fourth grader in a school near our house, and it is dated December 1969.

I Am a Belly Button

I am a belly button. I belong to a fat man. My name is Jay. Now I don't like the fat man I belong to. I don't like all the tall tall hairs or when the fat man slaps me. So one night when everybody was asleep I rolled off the fat man and rolled out of the door. I rolled into another house and found a pretty girl asleep. I rolled onto her and rolled beside her belly button. When she woke up she screamed. When the fat man woke up he was scared. Finally the fat man found out what had happened and he went over to the girl's home and got me back.

What crisp writing! What suspense! How vivid! The sad thing about it is, I think, that the teacher recognized no talent in it. Her sole comment was, "A weird story, David, and I think in bad taste."

519. At the turn of the century, a clever, word-and-worldly-wise fifth grader was asked to write an essay on men. She wrote:

Men are what women marry. They drink and smoke and swear, but don't go to church. Perhaps if they wore bonnets they would. They are more logical than women, also more zoological. Both men and women sprang from monkeys, but the women sprang further than the men.

520. Some years ago, *The Sentinel* of Milwaukee had a "My Pop's Tops" contest for children. There were some choice items, which ought to make any Pop feel great. Here are a few:

- "We have such good fun with my daddy that I wisht I had knew him sooner."

- "My Pop's Tops because he always takes good care of us children when my mother is in the hospital getting another. I have eight brothers and four sisters and know from experience."

- "He wants me to learn. Once he took me to Fence Lake and thrun me in to see if I could swim and I couldn't. He saved me, too."

- "I think all Pops are tops because if we didn't have Pops where would we be?"

- "He is a farmer. He smells like a cow and when I smell that cow in the house I know Pop is home and I am glad."

- "My Pop is tops because every time I ast him for a knickel he will start preeching that when he was a boy he had to earn his kenickls and at the same time he is putting his hand in his pocket and pulls out a kinckel, saying this is the last kinkel I have."

I can't think of a nobler way to finish this book than with a masterpiece—an unintended masterpiece—of kids' writing. I included it in my *A Treasury of Humor* (Prometheus Books, 1989), and it received more response from readers than any other item. Also, whenever I read it to school groups or conferences with whom I am consulting, I am always approached by people who ask, "Could you possibly let me have a copy of that 'owl' piece?"

Well, here it is, exactly as written by a fifth-grade girl. Notice its honesty, its ingenuity, the wonderful sentence variety, and the plain, frank, sophisticated humor. Also note that it is a superb try even though the author doesn't know anything about the subject.

521.

The Owl

The bird I am going to write about is an owl. I don't know much about the owl so I am going to write about the bat. The cow is a mammal. It has six sides, right, left, an upper and a lower. At the back it has a tail on which hangs the brush. With this it sends the flies away so they don't get in the milk.

The head is for the purpose of growing horns and so that the mouth can be somewhere. The horns are to butt with and the mouth is to eat with. Under the cow hangs the milk. The milk comes and there is never an end to the supply. How the cow does it I have not yet realized but it can make more and more.

The cow has a fine sense of smell and you can smell it far away. This is the reason for the fresh air in the country. The man cow is called an ox. It is not a mammal.

The cow does not eat much but what it eats it eats twice so that it gets enough. When it's hungry it moos and when it says nothing it's because its inside is full up.

The End

And "The End" of *Humorous Stories About the Human Condition*. If you should be hungry to use again any of the stories you have read here, don't moo. Instead, turn the page and use the indexes.

Subject Index

Note: Numbers in the indexes refer to story numbers, *not* page numbers.

abstinence, 216
academic meetings, 267
accents, 96, 97, 98
accidents, 165, 356, 422
acronyms, 119, 120
actions, good, 22
actors, 458
Adam and Eve, 369, 438, 496
adaptability, 460
administrative complexities, 297
admirals, 422
adultery, 151, 352
adulthood, 240
advertisements, 143
advertising, 398, 399, 400–403, 405
advice, 54, 162
African tribes, 302
aggression, 334
aging, 471
agnostics, 345
ain't, 59
airplanes, 19, 186, 270, 331
airports, 19
Alamo, 441
Albany (N.Y.) *Times Union,* 104
alcohol, 38, 272
alliteration, 309, 367
allowances, 203
ambassadors, 283
Amen!, 340
American Friends Service Committee, 423
American Museum of Natural History (N.Y.), 437
Americans, 7, 126
American sex, 512
anatomy, 83, 307, 508
angels, 336, 360
anger, 8, 13, 153, 154, 265, 482
animal sizes, 439
answers, 323; smart, 200, 394, 413
anthropology, 519
Anti-Saloon League, 38
Anti-Vice League, 38
anus, 207
anxiety, 51
appeals, 296
applause, 314
apologies, 395
archaeologists, 235
architecture, 389, 498
arguments, 11, 172, 173, 174, 215
arithmetic, 67, 69, 407, 432, 433, 435
art, 496; modern, 503
art classes, 500
artists, 327, 504
art work, 51
assumptions, unfounded, 1, 2
astrology, 126

SUBJECT INDEX

atheism, 347
atheists, 337, 346, 354, 492
Athens, 4
attention, paying, 58
aunts, 15
Australians, 5
authors, 516
autographs, 250, 381
Awbury Arboretum Association, 396
awkward age, 181

babbling, 326
babies, 66
bad day, 251
bad language, 165
bald eagle, 447
baldness, 160
ballet, 495
bananas, 39
bandits, 299
bank tellers, 384
Baptists, 376
bargaining, 382
bargains, 407, 408
barking, 18
baseball, 66, 85, 265, 394
bat, 521
bath lotions, 402
bathroom passes, 517
bathrooms, 499
batting practice, 265
beaches, 219
beans, 190
beards, 386
beauty, 220, 317, 510
bedbugs, 395
Bedlam, 132
beer, 491
begging, 10
behavior, childish, 151
behinds, 93
belief into action, 340
belly buttons, 518

Berlin Wall, 397
better halves, 342
Bible, 320, 329, 330, 332, 334, 350, 352, 375, 378, 409, 438
Bible study, 350
big-city dangers, 12
bigotry, 107
Bikini atoll, 14
Bill of Rights, 121
biology, 68
The Birmingham News, 512
birth, 207
birth control, 216
birthday presents, 461
black eyes, 11
black holes, 245
blindness, 91
bliss ninny, 114
Bloomingdale's, 477
blue whales, 439
boastfulness, 5
boasting, 29, 405
boat-building, 229
body parts, 83
boniprops, 109
bookkeepers, 257
Book of Revelation, 350
books, 145, 162, 169, 230, 257, 258, 507
boredom, 131, 136, 301, 497
boring talk, 149
Boston, 224, 441
Boston College, 349
Boston Tea Party, 442
boys, 144, 158, 319
Boys' Clubs, 383
boys, naughty, 144
Braille, 214
brevity, 301, 302, 303, 304, 309, 451
bridesmaids, 177
British, 6, 23, 283, 450, 490
British Empire, 442
British politics, 282
Broadway, 497

SUBJECT INDEX   213

builders, 389
bullrushes, 204
bulls and heifers, 212
bulletin boards, 80, 81
bureaucracy, 271, 294
burial, 344, 399
bus fares, 13
business, 391, 393–395, 404, 407, 410–415, 417, 446, 448
businessmen, 137, 192, 409
business problems, 389
business tricks, 400, 401
butcheries, 403
butchers, 255

cabins, log, 452
Calcutta, 28
California, 144, 440
Cambridge University, 17, 457
cameras, Kodak, 414
camps, summer, 262
Canada, 126
cannibals, 450
care, 233
cars, fast, 246; stalled, 266; used, 408
cathedrals, 364
Catholic Church, 227, 326
Catholics, 339, 342, 358, 363, 364, 365
caterpillar, 314
cats, 210, 368
caution, 514
ceilings, 3
celebrations, 415
celibacy, 45, 342
cemeteries, 64, 140, 236, 399, 473, 492
censorship, 121
census, 292
chair, 112
challenges, 89, 163
chameleons, 68
change (money), 385

chaos, 36, 502, 503
character building, 187
charity, 321, 513
Chatham Hall (Va.), 100
chastity, 513
cheating, 170, 379
chicken, Col. Sanders', 456
child-rearing, 145
children, 4, 79, 84, 156, 181, 182, 188, 196, 197, 199, 203, 429, 487, 496; bad, 4, 167; common sense of, 495; spoiled, 430. *See also,* kids, smart
children's writing, 4, 452, 475, 517–519, 521
Chinese, 98, 125
choirs, 357
chores, 168
Christ, bride(s) of, 363, 364
Christianity, 347, 353
Christmas, 283, 374
chrysanthemums, 263
church(es), 116, 183, 206, 321, 323, 324, 342, 379
church attendance, 355
church bulletin boards, 356, 357
church bulletins, 355
circuses, 437
citizenship, 425; American, 443
civilization, 457, 485
cleanliness, 170
clergymen, 361. *See also,* ministers, preachers, priests
clichés, 510
climate, 31
closets, 244
clocks, 306
clothes, 193; new, 152
clubs, 502
clumsiness, 147
clutter, 244
coaches, 139, 265, 392; football, 250, 465
coat racks, 63

SUBJECT INDEX

codes, light, 208
coffee breaks, 188
coffins, 398
coherence, 521
Columbia University, 123
comfort, 23, 416
commander-in-chief, 424
Commandments. See Ten Commandments
commencement, 310
comments, clever, 14
commercials, 324
committees, 112, 117
common sense, 59, 429
communication, 1, 2, 419
company, good, 31
competence, 146
competition, 403, 409
complaints, 395
compliments, 65, 157
computers, 94, 97
conceit, 457
concentration, 162
conception, 228
conciseness, 509
conclusions, 304
Concord Academy, 313
condensation (writing), 511
conferences, executive, 404
confidence, false, 32
confidentiality, 164
confusion, 100, 156, 189, 478
Congregational Church, 355
Congressmen, 279
conscientious objectors, 423. See also, pacifists
conservatism, 353
consideration, 28
consultants, 484
contributions, 365, 383
cooking, 166, 189, 190
cooperation, 12
Cooper Hospital (N.J.), 296
copyright, 230

cougars, 207
counseling, 343
counselors, marriage, 491; sex, 218
Country School (Madison, Conn.), The, 76
court, contempt of, 300, 482
courtship, 208
cows, 69, 521
Creation, The, 163, 348, 369, 390
credit, 491
creditors, 386
cremation, 399
cricket (game), 479
crime, 10, 107
criminals, 298
criticism (literary), 505, 515
cruelty, 476
crying, 181
curiosity, 206, 270
curses, 257
cuspidors, 86
customs duty, 45
cyberphobia, 243
cynicism, 284
Czechs, 252

dancing, 502
danger(s), 10, 14, 208, 269
dates (courtship), 211, 213
daughter. See relations, father-daughter
day, bad, 251
Dead Sea Scrolls, 512
deafness, 39, 470
death, 2, 64, 170, 201, 281, 293, 344, 345, 361, 398, 448, 472, 478, 513; life after, 343, 406
debates, 9
deception, 208
dedication, 162
deer, 285
defense, 281
degentrification, 484
democracy, 57, 207

SUBJECT INDEX 215

Democrats, 276, 277
dentists, 76, 397
depression (mental), 240
Depression, Great, 229
Detroit, 359
Devil, the, 338, 360
diapers, 66, 182
diaries, 196
dictatorship, 57
diet, 25
differences, 228
dillydallying, 175
dinosaurs, 439
disasters, 146, 147
discipline, 15, 36, 56, 316
discouragement, 314
discovery, 197
diseases, 216, 240
dishonesty, 42, 397, 406, 411, 431
disobedience, 427
distress, 241
divorce, 177
doctor, of philosophy, 123
doctors, 101, 135, 240, 463, 483
do-gooders, 22
dogs, 18, 118, 143, 158, 170, 249, 489
do-it-yourself, 169
doors, 86
doubters, 2
drinking, 159, 415, 463, 473
drunkenness, 64, 346, 478
dry cleaning, 376
dying, 473
dyslexia, 354

eagle, bald, 447
earth, 245, 254, 396
earthquakes, 144
earthworms, 430
Easter, 374
economics, 126, 229
ecumenism, 361
Eden, Garden of, 496

editors, 8, 511, 513
education, 52, 53, 55, 57–59, 62, 65, 68–81, 100, 120, 128, 226, 318, 452, 454–456, 515, 517, 518
efficiency, 373
Egypt, Hebrews' flight from, 329
eight-hundred (800) numbers, 176
ejaculations, 208
elderly, 1. *See also*, old age; senility
electrical systems, 464
elephants, 285
Emancipation Proclamation, 286
embarrassment, 500
embroidery, 214
emergencies, 68, 312
emotion, 164
encouragement, 213
England, 442; way of life, 493
English, 97, 126; good, 132
English as a second language, 96
enterprise, 436, 452
entrepreneurs, 381, 382
environment, 376
erasers, 93
essays, 452
etiquette, 484, 485, 487
eulogies, 513
euphemisms, 168
European Economic Community (E.E.C.), 291
evaluation, 61
Eve, 369, 438, 496
evidence, 300, 349
evils, 235
evolution, 163
exaggeration, 60, 153
examinations, 474
exceptions, 56
excrement, 1
excuses, 71, 72, 168, 169, 183, 310, 406
executives, 34, 394, 404
exercise, 209
expediters, 192

experience, 464
expertise, 290
explanations, 70
exploitation, 67, 155
expression, freedom of, 121
eye for an eye, 330

faith, 325, 414
faking, 411
fame, 315, 506
family friction, 148
family life, 382
family relations, 144, 145, 152, 430, 454, 488, 520. See also, relations
family visits, 161
famine, 44; Bengal, 423
fares, 431
farmers, 212, 412
farmhands, 290
farms, 69
farting, 489
fathers, 66, 124. See also, relations, father-daughter; father-son
fear, 79, 223, 503
federal offenses, 171
feel, 233
females, fierce, 15
feminism, 43
Ferdinand the Bull, 96
fighting, 16
fights, 184, 320, 330
fillings, 76
filling stations. See gas stations
film stars, 50
finding things, 189, 194
fireflies, 208
fishermen, 248
fishing, 146
flags, 380
flamingoes, 501
Flat Earth Society, 245
flattery, 108, 315
flat tires, 71, 135

flies, 3, 433
flight attendants, 19, 186
flowers, 400
flying, 19
food, 25. See also, health food
foolishness, 246
fools, 1, 40, 131
football, 36, 139, 390. See also, coaches, football
forecasters, 336
forefathers, 459
forgetfulness, 395
forgiveness, 205, 365
franchise, 275
frankness, 76
fraternal organizations, 443
freedom, 36. See also, expression, freedom of
Free Library of Philadelphia, 256
French, 6, 118, 129, 283
friendliness, 124
Friends' Central School (Philadelphia, Pa.), 341
friendship, 21, 158, 319
fruit, crystallized, 283
fucking. See intercourse
fundamentalists, 331
fundraising, 377-379, 383
funerals, 399, 406, 478
future, the, 201

gadgets, 197
galaxies, 245
gallantry, 43
gambling, 426
games, 470
Garden of Eden. See Eden, Garden of
gardens, 268
gas stations, 135, 401
gays. See men, gay
gender, 129, 180
generalizatons, 6
gentlemen, 134, 477, 485

geography, 325
Germans, 6, 283
Germantown Friends School (Philadelphia, Pa.), 53, 233
gestures, 372
gifts, 283
giraffes, 209
girlfriends, 222
glances, 15
gobbledegook, 293, 309
God, 125, 322, 326, 335–337, 347, 348, 354, 358, 369, 371, 474, 496
Golden Rule, 320, 334
goldfish, 416
golf, 26, 253, 254
gorillas, 285
gossip, 418
government forms, 292
government offices, 271
goverment regulations, 291
grace (prayer at meal), 328
grades, 72, 198, 226; passing, 407
grammar, 59, 84, 85, 87, 89, 91, 92, 129, 224, 317, 434, 481
Grand Canyon, 196
grandchildren, 180, 322
grandfathers, 180
grandmothers, 161
grapevine, 418
grasshoppers, 5
grocers, 67
guesses, 401
guests, 488
guns, 10

hack writers, 505
had, 89
hair, 160
half-wits, 312
Hamlet, 505
hands, 163
handshaking, 286
hanging, 298, 299
happiness, 202

Harrod's (London), 493
Harvard University, 60, 61, 81
hate, 185
Haverford College, 141
Hawaii, 450
health, 20, 25, 28
health food, 166
hearing aids, 470
hearsay, 300
heart, 83
heaven, 2, 6, 31, 205, 254, 345, 346, 474
Hebrew, 474
Hebrews' flight from Egypt, 329
heifers, 212
heirlooms, 147
hell, 6, 7, 13, 31, 256, 273, 346, 348, 357
helpfulness, 76
herbs, 402
heroes, 441, 452
Hindus, 366
hissing, 497
history, 425, 438, 442, 444, 446, 450, 453–456, 459
holdups (bank), 384
home-improvement, 194
homework, 67, 318
honesty, 45, 53, 143, 146, 147, 149, 181, 185, 318, 324, 328, 391, 411, 487, 506
horn-blowing, 266
hornets, 290
hospitals, 297, 363
hotels, 395
housekeeping, 189
House of Representatives, 287. *See also,* Congressmen
houses, 3
housework, 461
hugging, 20
human behavior, 28, 34, 36, 37, 39, 462
human beings, 3

218 SUBJECT INDEX

human body, 508
human relations, 26, 35, 391. *See also*, relations
humbugs, 445
humility, 29
humor, 24, 234, 312; Jewish, 362
hurry, 150, 166
husbands, 188
hypocrisy, 153

id, 342
ideals, 284
ideas, 350
ignorance, 118, 134
imagination, 318
immigrants, 443
immortality, 2
inauguration, Presidential, 56
inconspicuous, 307
indecency, 29
indexes, 155
infinitives, split, 87
inflexibility, 191
ingenuity, 46, 67, 73, 77, 84, 169, 407, 429, 431
inheritance, 198
inscriptions, 344, 501
insomniacs, 354
institutions, 1, 284
insults, 44, 131, 136, 137, 141, 160, 164, 173, 174, 194, 198, 199, 220, 221, 280, 282, 312, 315–317, 349, 371, 393, 428, 441, 483, 505
integration, 77
intelligence, 1
intercourse, 209, 212, 217, 222, 224
Internal Revenue Service (I.R.S.), 271, 293, 353, 379
international relations, 5, 283
intolerance, 368
introductions, 303, 304
inventions, 331, 337
inventors, 414

invitations, 486
Irish dialect, 289
Israel, 281
Israelites, 329

Japanese, 450
jargon, 58, 99, 100, 102, 103, 217, 296
Jews, 252, 335, 358, 363, 364, 366
Jews in the Bible, 444. *See also*, Hebrew, Israelites
job applications, 60
jobs, 239; worthless, 247
job-weariness, 52
jogging, 28, 335, 517
jokes, 202, 462
journalism, 514
Judaism, 22, 322
judges, 107, 171, 261, 301
junk, 244
juvenility, 151

kangaroos, 5
ketchup, 250
kidneys, 473
kids, smart, 436
kindergarten, 75, 76, 202
kindergarten teacher, 124
kindness, 494
King's English, 97
kisses, 461
Kodaks, 414

labeling, 121
labels, 189
laboratories, 33
ladies, 45, 477
Lancet (British medical journal), 307
landlords, 458
language, 73, 74, 82, 84–88, 91, 92, 95–98, 101–103, 105–111, 122, 124–130, 132–135, 147, 151, 154, 168, 217, 221, 278, 279,

SUBJECT INDEX   219

288, 289, 291, 292, 296, 301, 341, 400, 419–421, 427, 434, 471, 474, 479, 481, 508, 510–514, 519, 521; bad, 165; dirty, 130; military, 102
Latin, 94, 95, 257
laughter, 234
lawn mowers, 258
laws, 516
lawyers, 261, 301, 366, 483
laziness, 27, 30, 37, 46, 247
leadership, 34, 57, 392
leaks, 142
learning, 62
lectures, 54
Lent, 30
Lesbians, 215
lessons, 298
letters, 164; anonymous, 223; form, 296, 395; to the editor, 8
liars, 248, 375, 480
librarians, 256
libraries, 81, 256, 453
lies, 253
life, 235; enjoyment of, 183; goals of, 182; problems in, 8, 238, 360; signs of, 80
Life magazine, 506
life after death, 37
life expectancy, 293
light, speed of, 70
lightning, 464
Lincoln's Birthday, 453
lions, 285, 361
lipstick, 213
liquor, 246. *See also,* whiskey
listening, 11, 241, 420
literature, 128, 451, 505–507
living together, 122
logic, 32, 59, 64, 70, 74, 88, 160, 264, 279, 299, 434
long-windedness, 136, 305, 306, 308, 309
looks, come hither, 211; stay-thither, 211
loss of things, 194
lotus-eaters, 114
love, 47, 156, 179, 185, 233, 235
love-making, 215. *See also,* intercourse
luxury, 4
lying, 71, 199, 274

machines, talking, 303
Magna Carta, 444
maids, 46
Maine, 405
malaprops, 109
male chauvinist pigs, 43
managers, 393
manners, 4, 17, 28, 38, 43, 394, 442, 476, 477, 479, 480, 485, 486, 488, 490
manure, 130
marketing, 25
marriage, 122, 171–174, 176–179, 188, 191–193, 235
marriage, problems in, 195, 343. *See also,* counselors, marriage
marriage license, 225
masochism, 362
Massachusetts Institute of Technology, 94, 305
mating, 68
Matthew, Book of, 375
maturity, 188
meaning, 91
meat slicers, 255
medical care, 101
memberships, 383
memory, 310
men, 90, 519; fat, 518; gay, 215; old, 462–464. *See also,* relations, men vs. women
menus, 250, 260
metaphors, 101, 314, 510
metaphors, mixed, 103, 104, 105, 278

Methodists, 376
mice, 174. See also, mouse
Michigan, politics in, 288
Michigan, University of, 7, 34
migrations, 231
military, the, 419, 422–424, 426–428, 456
Milwaukee Sentinel, 520
ministers, 176, 206, 272, 332, 333, 342, 373, 375, 483
miracles, 483
misbehavior, 186
misery, 236, 262
mistakes, 32, 235, 395, 436
mistresses, 17
misunderstanding, 1, 2, 124
mitzvahs, 22
modern times, 176. See also, art, modern; music, modern
modesty, 21, 451
mole, 426
Mona Lisa, 446
monasteries, 257. See also, monks
money, 103, 193, 378, 385; appeals for, 117; earning, 203; wasting, 246
monks, 367. See also, monasteries
monotony, 190
Morris Arboretum (Philadelphia, Pa.), 285
motels, 42, 249
mothers, 145, 156, 157, 203. See also, relations, mother-son
mothers-in-law, 161, 164
motivation, 48, 49, 51, 54, 417, 515
Mount Sinai School of Medicine, 471
mourning, 170
mouse, 209. See also, mice
mufflers, 388
mules, 173
mumble, 295
museums, 437
music, bad, 134; modern, 502

music critics, 132
mystery, 509

nagging, 192
naïveté, 159, 237, 475
names, 74, 167, 449
National Archives (Washington, D.C.), 492
naturalists, 445
Nebraska, 484
necking, 47
negative approach, 167
negotiations, 352
neighborhoods, 319
neighbors, 27
nepotism, 410
Netherlands, 380
New England Journal of Medicine, 296
New Hampshire, 373
newspapers, 511
New Year's resolutions, 30
New York, 13
New Yorker, The, 24, 506
New York Public Library, 256
Noah's Ark, 389, 501
nonsense, scribbling, 268
Northwest Mutual, The, 418
noses, runny, 47
nuclear bombs, 14
nude (posing), 500
nudity, 193, 219, 500.
numbers, 247
nuns, 363, 364
nurses, 297
nursing homes, 468, 469
Nutcracker Suite, The, 495

obesity, 44, 240
obfuscation, 295
objections, 261
objectivity, 78
obscenity, 121
observation, 76

office boys, 394
old age, 1, 219, 468-472, 474, 475.
    See also, men, old; women, old
Old South, 142
Old Testament, 444
one-minute paper, 61
only, 92
opinions, 40
optimism, 338
orators, 308
orders, 158, 419, 424, 427
organization(s), 276, 284, 290, 414, 418
organizing, 179
originality, 435
overcharging, 135
overpopulation, 231, 232
overwork, 169
owl, 521

pacifists, 353, 455
palindromes, 127
pancreas, 510
panties, 214
paradise, 2, 268
parenting, 186, 187
parents, 81, 187; working, 166
parking, 333
parking lots, 16
parrots, 259
parsonages, 342
parties, 38, 195, 488, 489; dinner, 328. See also, political parties
pastoral visits, 323
pathways, 498
patience, 150
patriotism, 113, 377, 403, 444, 447
peace, breach of, 479
pearls before swine, 52
penis(es), 219, 270
Pennsylvania, University of, 396
pens, 95
people, odd, 242; size of, 282
pep talks, 139

perfection, 339
permits, learner's, 225
persistence, 48
personnel managers, 416
perspective, 3, 182, 439, 454, 456, 457, 472, 475; lack of, 1, 2
pets, 172
Pharoah's daughter, 204
Ph.Ds, 123
Philadelphia, 106, 442
Philadelphia City Council, 285
Philadelphia Zoo, 285
philosophers, 4, 178, 187
philosophy, 351
phobias, 243
photography, 157
physical fitness, 219, 393
physicists, 267
picketing, 353
pictures, class, 201
pilots, 19
planning, 103, 177, 182, 498
plays, bad (theater), 497
pleasure(s), 210, 465
poets, 386
poison, 280
Poles, 252
police, 41, 107, 332, 333, 516
politeness, 28, 487
political parties, 276
politicians, 103, 273, 274, 288
politics, 105, 130, 272, 275, 278-282, 285-287, 289, 410
polyester, 501
Pope, the, 227
population, 247
population explosion, 232
portraits, 446, 504
posing, 500
postcards, 262
potatoes, 373
poverty, 140
practicality, 67, 170, 386, 461, 498
praise, 83

prayer(s), 150, 183, 323, 325–327
praying mantis, 208
preachers, 125, 340, 372, 374, 376
predators, 208
pregnancy, 216, 509
Presbyterians, 342
Presidents (U.S.), 507
pressure, 379
pride, 425
priests, 45, 326, 342, 346, 365
Princeton University, 267
priorities, 423
prisons, 492
privileges, 294
problems, 176, 236, 249, 251. See also, life, problems in; world problems
procrastination, 54, 115
procrastinators, 137
prodigies, 494
professors, 61, 123, 141
profits, 397
progress, 459, 460; lack of, 4
promiscuity, 223
promptness, 175
pronunciation, 421
proof, 349
prosperity, 308
prostitutes, 82, 221, 222, 246
Protestants, 358
prudence, 16
Psalm, Twenty-Third, 116
Psalm 1989, 116
psychiatrists, 241, 242
puberty, 185
punctuation, 90
punishment(s), 298, 427, 428
puns, 445
Puritans, 368
purposefulness, 417

Quakers, 29, 335, 459
quarrels, 193
questions, 133; difficult, 62; good, 199; naive, 239
quitting, 48
quitting time, 37

rabbit, 2
racism, 77
railroad men, 213
railroads, 251, 405
rain, 142, 336
raises, 415, 416
rallies, political, 277
rats, 65
realism, 48, 50, 60, 85, 184, 290, 320, 432, 433, 447, 458
reason, 337, 460; lack of, 9
rebuffs, 212
recognition, 49
record players, 303
rectories, 342
Red Sea, 329, 335
regulations, 292, 297
relations, 173; father-daughter, 159; father-son, 146; girls vs. boys, 184; male vs. female, 197; married, 175; men vs. women, 16; mother-son, 154. See also, international relations
religion, 2, 322, 325–327, 329–339, 341–353, 355–361, 363–371, 374–378, 444, 474; retail and wholesale, 341
reminiscing, 201
Renaissance art, 499
rent, 458
report cards, 72, 226
reporters, 288, 514
reproduction, 68, 230
Republicans, 277
requests, stupid, 237
research, 78
restaurants, 111, 250; greasy spoon, 260
restrooms, 270
retirement, 465

SUBJECT INDEX

retirement homes, 475
retorts, 1, 2, 44, 151, 175, 221, 254, 280, 333, 346, 348, 349, 370, 373, 376, 385, 390, 392, 428, 463, 477, 481, 488, 489, 504; clever, 63
reunions, class, 31
Revelation, Book of, 350
revenge, 18, 155, 330, 470
rewards, 49
rhetoric, 9
rhinoceroses, 414
riddles, 133, 299, 449
ridicule, 24
risks, 414
robbery, 12
rock walls, 264
romance, 47, 466
roses, 263
Rotary Club, 342
roué, 246
Royal Shakespeare Company, 505
rules, 36, 56, 258, 297, 490, 517
rumors, 418

safaris, 361
safety, 356
salaries, 415
sales meetings, 392
Salisbury Cathedral (U.K.), 444
salmon, 231
sarcasm, 186, 266, 486
satire, 24
savage, 90
scattering, 252
scholars, 55, 64
school boards, 79
school principals, 57, 81
schools, 51, 200; parochial, 339
science, 65, 70, 78, 200, 491
Scilly Isles (U.K.), 268
scolding, 198
Scotch, 126
scrod, 224

seagull, 1
second-graders, 53
security, 104
seepage, 399
self-confidence, 200, 339
self-esteem, 405
self-evaluation, 53
self-worship, 35
senility, 1, 468, 469
senior citizens, 13
septic tank trucks, 388
sermons, 125, 324, 326, 340, 357, 371, 372
sex, 2, 129, 208, 210, 219, 226, 227, 232; American, 512; hot, 218
sex appeal, 50
sex counselors. *See* counselors, sex
sex education, 207, 233
sexism, 111, 112, 129
sexual attraction, 229
sexual intercourse. *See* intercourse
sexuality, 45, 214, 221, 230, 512
sharing, 350
sharks, 483
shaving, 193
sheep, 279, 432
Sheltren College (Cape May, N.J.), 63
sheriffs, 272
shopping, 25, 193, 477
shouting, 371
shorthand, 400
shrews, 178
sight-seeing, 359
sign, no smoking, 493
signs, 268–271, 347, 359, 387, 388, 393, 491–493, 516
silence, 81, 387
sin, 205, 206, 376
Sinai, Mount, 352
sinners, 339
Sistine Chapel (Rome), 327
Six-day War, 281
skepticism, 204, 349

SUBJECT INDEX

skiing, 491
slang, 126, 130
sleep, 18, 307
slogans, 81, 94
smoking, 218, 463
sneezing, 217
snobbery, 315, 481
sociology, 90
soul, 508
souvenir stores, 397
Soviet Union, 252, 287, 294
Spanish, 96
spawning, 231
speakers, 302, 303-306, 308-312, 314, 315
speaking, 93
Spectator, The, 508
speech, 21
speeches, 108, 274, 372; dull, 309; subjects for, 313
speeding, 41, 332
spelling, 75, 88, 262, 263
spigots, 499
spilling, 168
spinsters, 210
spitting, 196
spouse, faithful, 179
spying, 252
squandering, 246
"Star Spangled Banner," 113, 377
stationery store, 95
station wagons, 148
statistics, 247, 440
stories, 509
storms, dust, 138
streaking (nude), 500
stress, 150
stupidity, 1, 419
substitutes, 82
succeeding, 48, 78
success, 78
suffrage, women's, 275
suicide, 25
sun, 70, 245

Sunday School(s), 204, 205, 320, 329, 369, 370, 496
superintendents, 51
supermarkets, 43
Supreme Court, 171
surgery, 363
surprises, 190, 316, 328
survey, 283
suspense, 509
swearing, 86, 181, 265
symbols, 447
systems, 189

tact, 41, 154, 165, 221, 480, 489
Taft School (Watertown, Conn.), 56
Tahoe, Lake, 440
tailors, 390
talk, boring, 149
talking, 11, 97, 149, 287, 420
Tallahassee (Fla.) *Democrat,* 105
taxes, 99, 102, 380, 442; income, 253
taxi drivers, 224
tea, 280, 442; benefits of, 23
teachers, 50, 51, 75, 79, 82, 93, 201, 316, 317, 408, 432-435, 518
teaching, 49, 61, 62, 66, 69, 70, 73, 74, 81
teaching methods, 71
technology, modern, 329
teenagers, 146, 152, 225, 238, 503
teeth, 478
telephone service, 237
temper, 174
temperance, 280
temptation, 333
tempus fugit, 95
Ten Commandments, 8, 330, 352, 511
tennis, 467
tenses, 317
tests, 71, 325
test scores, 51
Texans, 5, 441

SUBJECT INDEX 225

theft, 42, 249; car, 12
theology, 351
thinking, 61, 160, 234
thinness, 44
threats, 10, 19, 193, 223
"Three Blind Mice," 476
tickets, 332
time-savers, 404
tips, 491
titles, 412
toasts, 451
toilets, 377
tolerance, 358
toll booths, 385
tombs, 140
tombstones, 344, 501
Tommies, 421
tooth extraction, 397
tourists, 7
tragedy, 362, 466
trains, 431
translations, 96, 128
travel, 136
trespasses, 333
trials, 261, 300, 301, 480, 482
trickery, 46
tricks, 170, 327, 426, 445
trigonometry, 107
tripod, 307
trips, 148
triskaidekaphobia, 243
trout, 248
trucks, 429
trust, 391
truth, 45, 71, 91, 248, 261, 274, 480
turkeys, 447

uglification, 220
umpires, 476
understatement, 2
undertakers, 399, 448
underwear, 29
United States Government, 287
universe, 245

urination, 197
U.S.S.R. *See* Soviet Union

vacations, 33, 56, 148
vagina, 207
vanity, 35
variety, 190
vegetables, fresh, 27
vehicles, 516
verbosity, 141
Vesuvius, Mount, 7
vice-presidency, 289
victory, 426
view, short-range, 182
violence, 9, 36
violinists, 494
vocabulary, 85, 115
voices, 15
volcanoes, 7
vomiting, 321
voting, 273, 275

waiters, 111, 481
walkie-talkie, 329
Wall Street Journal, 99
warnings, 121
wars, 455
waste, medical, 296
watches, 306
water, 440
Waterloo, Battle of, 425
weather, 106, 335
weather forecasts, 138
whales, 439
whims, 191
whips, 290
whiskey, Scotch, 473
whistling, 183
White House, 286
wind, 264
winners, 16
wiping up, 168
wisdom, 40, 56, 80, 413; pearls of, 52

wisecracking, 24
wit, 24, 74
witnesses, 261, 480
wittiness, 80
women, 90, 519; formidable, 17; old, 461, 466, 467
women's rights, 280. See also, relations, men vs. women; suffrage, women's
word/food processors, 125
wordiness, 102, 291
words, 24, 85, 151; dangers of, 125; fancy, 115; four-letter, 233; the longest, 110
work, 33, 239; hard, 55; toughness of, 55

work rules, 384
world, flat, 229
world problems, 4, 390
World War I, 421, 457
worms, 490
writers, 54, 155
writing, 162, 509–511, 515, 516; student, 233. See also, children's writing.

yacht, Presidential, 425
Yale University, 9, 60, 305, 315
Ypres, 421

zoologists, 65

Index of Famous People and Celebrities

Adams, John Quincy, 507
Addison, Joseph, 508
Angell, James B., 34
Astor, Lady Nancy L., 280
Attila the Hun, 449

Bankhead, Tallulah, 235
Beard, Charles A., 123
Benchley, Robert, 506
Bernhardt, Sarah, 466
Boren, James H., 295
Brooks, Phillips, 345
Broun, Heywood, 274
Burns, George, 463
Burton, Robert, 55
Bush, Vannevar, 94

Caesar, Julius, 94
Calderone, Dr. Mary, 207
Carnegie, Andrew, 413
Charles, (Prince of Wales), 97
Chaucer, Geoffrey, 128
Cher (Sarkisian), 235
Chesterton, G. K., 44, 299
Christie, Agatha, 235
Churchill, Winston, 228, 280
Clemens, Samuel L. *See* Twain, Mark

Cook, James (captain), 450
Crockett, Davy, 441

Darwin, Charles, 445
Davis, William Morris, 234
Dayan, Moshe, 281
Dufy, Raoul, 504
Dunne, Peter Finley, 289

Eastman, George, 414
Edison, Thomas Alva, 33, 303
Einstein, Albert, 267
Eisenhower, Dwight David, 34, 456
Elizabeth II, Queen, 403
Elman, Mischa, 494
Esty, John C., Jr., 109

Fields, W. C., 48
Ford, Henry, 404
Frankfurter, Felix, 171
Franklin, Benjamin, 447
Frost, Robert, 264

George, David Lloyd, 282
George, Phyllis, 220
Gladstone, William Ewart, 23
Golden, Harry Lewis, 77
Grant, Ulysses S., 419

INDEX OF FAMOUS PEOPLE AND CELEBRITIES

Greene, Robert, 505
Gregorian, Vartan, 256

Harte, Bret, 513
Hoover, Herbert, 381, 507

Ingersoll, Robert G., 345
Inouye, Daniel, 450

James, William, 155
Jefferson, Thomas, 286
Jesus, 216, 327, 339, 359, 363
John, the Baptist, 449
Jonah, 271
Jonson, Beu, 505

Kerr, Jean, 510
Kettering, Charles F., 32
Kosygin, Alexei N., 252

Lamb, Charles, 22
Leacock, Stephen, 126
Lear, Edward, 367
Lewis, Sinclair, 315
Lincoln, Abraham, 279, 286, 452, 453, 507
Livingston, Dr. David, 133
Lombardi, Vince, 250
Longfellow, Henry Wadsworth, 257

Mary (mother of Jesus), 327
Masaryk, Thomas G., 252
Mead, Margaret, 49
Milton, John, 451
Moltke, von, Count Helmuth, 420
More, Thomas, 49
Moses, 204, 329, 335, 352
Muehl, William, 9, 36
Mumford, Lewis, 179

Nash, Ogden, 208
Nietzsche, Friedrich Wilhelm, 347
Noah, 336

Parker, Dorothy, 24, 131
Paul, St., 81
Peale, Norman Vincent, 236
Pershing, John J., 397
Peter, St., 273
Pilsudski, Joseph, 252
Protagoras, 81

Raphael (Raffaello Santi), 449
Reagan, Ronald, 507
Revere, Paul, 441
Rogers, Will, 276
Roosevelt, Theodore, 286, 507
Rousseau, Jean Jacques, 49
Ruth, George Herman ("Babe"), 381, 387

Safire, William, 109
Shakespeare, William, 344, 451, 505
Shaw, George Bernard, 44, 88, 132, 227, 460, 486, 492
Shepherd, Cybill, 220
Sheridan, Richard Brinsley, 109
Smith, Jaclyn, 220
Socrates, 4, 49, 178
Stanley, Henry Morton, 133
Stevens, Thaddeus, 482
Stevenson, Adlai Ewing (b. 1900), 108

Taft, Horace Dutton, 56
Taft, William Howard, 56
Tennyson, Alfred Lord, 451
Thurber, James, 24
Truman, Harry S., 130, 424
Twain, Mark, 31, 258, 448, 451

Ussher, James (bishop), 348
Ustinov, Peter, 187

Vinci, da, Leonardo, 446

Washington, Booker T., 81
Washington, George, 253, 337, 444

INDEX OF FAMOUS PEOPLE AND CELEBRITIES

West, Mae, 235
Wilde, Oscar, 134
Wilson, Woodrow, 507
Wodehouse, P. G., 15, 162

Wright, Orville, 331
Wright, Wilbur, 331

Zappa, Frank, 121